Leading Organizational Change in a Recession

Leading Organizational Change in a Recession

The Role of Transformational Leadership

Linus Ochai

EXCELLER BOOKS®
A GLOBAL PRESS

Leading Organizational Change in a Recession:
The Role of Transformational Leadership

Cover by Exceller Books using resources from Pixabay.com

ISBN: 978-93-48892-49-2

First published in India in 2025 by Exceller Books,
An imprint of GE Group
G1, Dream Apartment, Degree College Road, Belgharia,
Kolkata, 700056, India
www.excellerbooks.com

EXCELLER BOOKS®
A GLOBAL PRESS

Dedication

To my mother, Mrs. Salimetu Ochai, a leader by nature.

Acknowledgement

I am grateful to God for the gift of life and his grace that made this book a reality. My appreciation goes to my mentor, Pastor Simeon Afolabi and his dear wife, Pastor (Mrs.) Ruth Afolabi for their impact in my life and ministry. I deeply appreciate my wife, Florence and my daughter, Joy for their companionship; and the entire Ochai's family for their love and support. Finally, I appreciate Exceller Books for publishing this book.

Table of Contents

Chapter 1 | Introduction

1.1. Background to the Study

According to Samuel C. Certo and Trevis Certo (2006) in their book *Modern Management*, leadership is defined as "the process of directing the behavior of others towards the accomplishment of some objectives." Directing, in this sense, means causing individuals to act in a certain way or follow a particular course. Ideally, this course is perfectly consistent with such factors as established organizational policies, procedures, and job descriptions. The central theme of leadership is getting things accomplished through people.

Tom Moriarty (2011) defines leadership as influencing the activities of others toward accomplishing a goal.

From the foregoing definitions, leadership is influence. It is the ability of the leader to galvanize both human and material resources toward the accomplishment of organizational objectives, which, among others, is to maximize profit and minimize loss. The average business owner or shareholder is keen on return on investment. To successfully lead an organization on the path to success, the leader must be familiar with what it takes to enforce changes that will make organizational success sustainable in the face of threats to the survival of the organization.

For instance, the COVID-19 pandemic has adversely affected the economies of many nations. Some economies are currently in a recession, generating a lot of panic in many organizations across the globe. Most managers have reacted by downsizing as the first step to staying afloat while exploring other survival strategies to keep the organization running.

According to World Bank Prospect Group Director Ayhan Kose (2020), "The COVID-19 recession is singular in many respects and is likely to be the deepest one in advanced economies since the Second World War and the first output contraction in emerging and developing economies in at least the past six decades." He further posited that "The current episode has already seen by far the fastest and steepest downgrades in global growth forecasts on record. If the past is any guide, there may be further growth downgrades in store, implying that policymakers may need to be ready to employ additional measures to support activity."

The World Bank, in its June 2020 *Global Economic Prospects*, revealed that "The swift and massive shock of the coronavirus pandemic and shutdown measures to contain it have plunged the global economy into a severe contraction." According to World Bank forecasts, the global economy will shrink by 5.2% this year. That would represent the deepest recession since the Second World War, with the largest fraction of economies experiencing declines in per capita output since 1870.

According to *Channels Television*, Nigeria's Finance Minister, Mrs. Zainab Ahmed, while speaking on the latest GDP figures released by the National Bureau of Statistics (NBS) about the current recession in the country at the ongoing 26th Nigerian Economic Summit—organized by the Nigerian Economic Summit Group (NESG) and the Federal Ministry of Finance, Budget, and National Planning—said the COVID-19-induced recession followed the pattern seen across the world, where many countries had entered an economic recession.

Ahmed said, "Nigeria is not alone in this, but I will say that Nigeria has outperformed all of these economies in terms of the record of negative growth."

The country's economy posted a second consecutive negative growth, contracting by 3.62% in the third quarter.

This negative growth is much better than the 6.01% that was earlier forecasted by the NBS.

The reality is that organizations do go through crises that may threaten their existence as entities. Such crises may arise from natural disasters, a pandemic like COVID-19, competition, the changing nature of customer loyalty, the inability to cope with the pace of technological development, and a lack of flexibility to adapt to change. Having said this, it is important to note that the greatest crises that confront organizations—both for-profit and nonprofit alike—occur during a recession. When there is a recession in an economy, it affects the purchasing power of the average customer. There are usually job cuts and dwindling financial fortunes for businesses and governments.

At such critical moments, there is a need for the emergence of transformational leaders who can guide organizations through change, creatively managing the scarce resources available to keep the organization afloat and turning around its fortunes by ensuring profitability. Leaders who can steer an organization through a recession are great assets because they possess the rare combination of character, competence, and the ability to connect with an unmotivated team and inspire them to accomplish organizational objectives.

A classic example of leading organizational or national change during a recession can be seen in the history of Singapore, a nation that transformed from a third-world country to a first-world country in about 50 years. The story of Singapore's transformation—impacting its educational, political, and socio-economic development at all levels—can be traced to the quality of leadership provided by its Prime Minister, Lee Kuan Yew.

At independence in 1965, Singapore was grossly underdeveloped and lacked both natural and skilled human resources. In every sense of the word, it was an economy in recession. However, through the leadership skills of Lee Kuan Yew—who understood the power of change in an organization—Singapore rose from a recessed economy to become one of the strongest economies in the world today. It now has the fourth-highest per capita real income globally and boasts one of the best airlines and airports in the world.

The critical ingredients of leadership, as seen in the example of Lee Kuan Yew's transformational leadership, are service, innovation, education, advanced infrastructure, the rule of law, and the deployment of technology. The leadership style employed was a blend of semi-authoritarian and laissez-faire economic policies that allow tax exemptions, tax holidays, and low taxes on designated commodities.

Organizational change, as defined by Certo et al. (2006), is the process of modifying an existing organization to increase organizational efficiency, which is a measure of how an organization can achieve set objectives despite the obstacles posed by a recession. To make this concept of organizational change a reality, particularly during a recession, the leader must be courageous enough to swim against the tide by thinking outside the box and doing things that contradict the status quo. To lead successfully, the leader should consider strengthening organizational authority and ensuring flexibility in role allocation to team members based on identified relevant skill sets needed in crisis moments. It is important to establish clear lines of effective communication among team members and employ modern technology. Depending on the organization's financial viability, some leaders may consider the option of downsizing human resources to cut overhead costs.

It is pertinent to note that a key manifestation of a recession is a decline in economic activities due to a widespread drop in customer spending. The implication is that organizations producing goods and services suddenly discover that supply outweighs demand, which, in turn, leads to competition among organizations to meet the needs of a few customers who have purchasing power. This calls for innovation and creativity on the part of organizational leaders to minimize losses and maximize profits. Since the initial reaction of most managers in a recession is to downsize, there is a tendency for unemployment to rise rather sharply. This further impacts purchasing power negatively, slowing down the economy of the nation concerned.

What is needed to reposition an organization in a recession is bold transformational leadership.

1.2. Statement of General Problem

Organizations face challenges in a recessed economy. Such challenges range from poor customer patronage and dwindling revenue to poor returns on investment. In a recession, many organizations are unable to maximize profits because the customer's purchasing power is at its lowest level.

Most organizations react by downsizing and cutting costs to avoid going out of business. When there is a recession in an economy, it affects the purchasing power of the average customer. There are usually job cuts and dwindling financial fortunes for businesses and governments.

Conceptual Framework

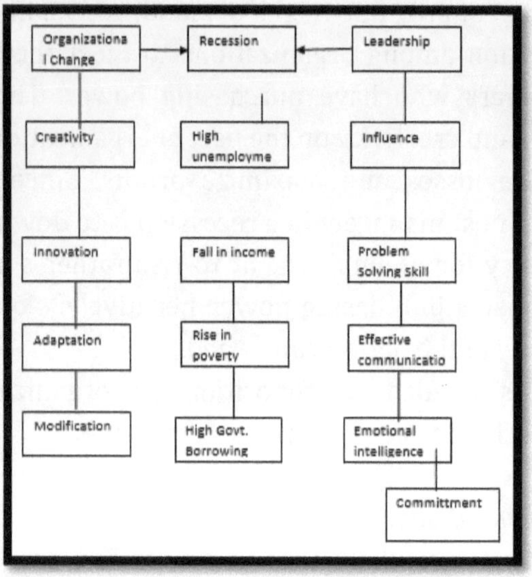

1.3. Objectives of the Study

The objective of this study is to investigate and emphasize the role of transformational leadership in steering the ship of an organization to safety during a recession. This work specifically aims to accomplish the following:

- The relationship between the influence of an organizational leader and recession.
- The relationship between the problem-solving skills of an organizational leader and recession.
- The relationship between the effective communication skills of an organizational leader and recession.
- The relationship between the emotional intelligence skills of an organizational leader and recession.
- The relationship between the commitment of an organizational leader and recession.
- The relationship between the creativity of an organizational leader and recession.

- The relationship between the innovation of an organizational leader and recession.
- The relationship between an organizational leader's ability to adapt to change and recession.
- The relationship between an organizational leader's ability to modify existing structures and recession.

1.4. Research Questions

- This research work seeks to answer the following research questions:
- To what extent does the influence of an organizational leader on team members help mitigate recession?
- To what extent do an organizational leader's problem-solving skills help mitigate recession?
- To what extent do the effective communication skills of an organizational leader help combat recession?
- To what extent do the emotional intelligence skills of an organizational leader help address recession?
- To what extent does the commitment of a leader assuage recession?
- To what extent does the creativity of an organizational leader mitigate recession?
- To what extent does the innovation of a leader curb recession?
- To what extent does an organizational leader's ability to adapt to change minimize the impact of recession?
- To what extent does an organizational leader's ability to modify existing organizational structures minimize the impact of recession?

1.5. Research Hypotheses

The following hypotheses are formulated by the researcher to investigate and emphasize the role of transformational leadership in steering the ship of an organization to safety during a recession. This study is based on the following assumptions:

- Ho1: There is no significant relationship between the influence of an organizational leader on his/her team members and recession.
- Ho2: There is no significant relationship between an organizational leader's problem-solving skills and recession.
- Ho3: There is no significant relationship between an organizational leader's effective communication skills and recession.
- Ho4: There is no significant relationship between an organizational leader's emotional intelligence skills and recession.
- Ho5: There is no significant relationship between an organizational leader's commitment and recession.
- Ho6: There is no significant relationship between an organizational leader's creativity and recession.
- Ho7: There is no significant relationship between an organizational leader's innovation and recession.
- Ho8: There is no significant relationship between an organizational leader's ability to adapt to change and recession.
- Ho9: There is no significant relationship between an organizational leader's ability to modify existing organizational structures and recession.

1.6. Significance of the Study

This study is significant in many ways to a wide range of stakeholders. It is valuable for organizational leaders as well as leaders in government. It is equally significant due to its relevance and practical application to team members who aspire to leadership positions and roles. Business leaders, their clients, investors, and the economy will benefit immensely from this study. It will enable them to be proactive in the face of recession and other crises that can potentially threaten their existence. Therefore, this study is significant in the following ways:

Organizational leaders will be equipped with the relevant leadership skills required to steer their organizations through the turbulence of a recession. They will understand the dynamics of innovation and creativity that transformational leaders need to make a difference in crisis situations, particularly in a recessed economy.

Organizational leaders in both for-profit and non-profit organizations will benefit immensely as they learn the problem-solving skills needed to address organizational challenges during a recession.

Leaders and team members will develop and deploy appropriate emotional intelligence skills required to collaborate effectively and meet organizational goals during crises, particularly in a recession.

Employers and investors will identify the relevant skills to look for in potential organizational leaders they intend to hire and empower. They will be able to choose dynamic transformational leaders who have the capacity to aggregate relevant human, material, and financial resources to meet organizational goals, make decisions that maximize profit, and minimize losses during a recession.

The government will benefit from the skills and expertise of business leaders who possess the knowledge and ability to add value to the economy during a recession. Responsible governments provide some form of palliatives or bailouts to organizations that have the leadership acumen to manage resources efficiently, minimizing job losses and positively impacting the economic outcome of a nation during a recession.

Policy makers and educational institutions will benefit from this study as it will help them formulate and implement policies that strengthen leadership studies. This includes developing a curriculum that imparts relevant leadership skills needed by leaders in the workforce—critical skills required before, during, and after a recession.

Clients will benefit from the transformational leadership experience of organizational leaders who can sustain production, implement a sustainable marketing strategy, and maintain customer loyalty during a recession. The character and competence of organizational leadership in times of crisis determine the confidence or lack thereof that clients have in an organization.

The economy benefits tremendously from the leadership prowess of business leaders who possess the requisite skills to steer their organizations successfully, conduct business transactions that positively impact the economy, and mitigate the adverse effects of a recession.

1.7. Scope of the Study

The scope of this study, *Leading Organizational Change in a Recession*, focuses on the COVID-19-induced recession of 2020. With the advent of COVID-19 and the attendant layoff of workers by some organizations, as well as the eventual lockdown of many economies, the International Monetary Fund projected a deep global recession in 2020, with global economies expected to shrink by 4.4%. While speaking at the IMF's World Economic Forum in Boston, the IMF Chief Economist, Gita Gopinath (2020), stated that the pandemic had shut down businesses and industries around the globe.

In their write-up, *"COVID-19-Induced Recession: Biggest Economic Policy Challenge for Austria in the 'Second Republic'"*, Gerhard Fenz et al. (2020) stated that the lockdown measures adopted to contain the COVID-19 pandemic had sent economies worldwide into a deep recession.

According to Channels Television, Nigeria's Finance Minister, Mrs. Zainab Ahmed, while speaking on the latest GDP figures released by the National Bureau of Statistics (NBS) about the current recession in the country at the ongoing 26th Nigerian Economic Summit—organized by the Nigerian Economic Summit Group (NESG) and the Federal Ministry of Finance, Budget, and National Planning—said that the COVID-19-induced recession followed the pattern seen across the world, where many countries had entered an economic recession.

The scope of this study also focuses on organizational leaders in five for-profit organizations and five not-for-profit organizations. The sample size for questionnaire administration in these organizations is 100. As such, questionnaires will be administered to ten top management leaders in each organization. The organizations involved in this study are:

- Firstlove Assembly, Port Harcourt
- Jevinik Restaurant, Port Harcourt
- Rehoboth Health & Emergency Response, Port Harcourt
- Technip FMC, Port Harcourt
- M Praise Yoghurts, Port Harcourt
- Sterling Bank, Rumuola Branch, Port Harcourt
- International Health Management Services, Port Harcourt
- Total Nigeria PLC, Port Harcourt
- Rivers State Ministry of Works, Port Harcourt

1.8. Definition of Terms

All the following definitions are taken from the *Oxford Advanced Learner's Dictionary*:

- Recession: A period of reduced economic activity.
- Crisis: A time of great danger, difficulty, or doubt when problems must be solved or important decisions must be made.
- Economy: The relationship between production, trade, and the supply of money in a particular country or region.
- Creativity: The use of skill and imagination to produce something new or to create art.
- Innovation: The introduction of new things, ideas, or ways of doing something.
- Transformation: A complete change in somebody or something.
- Organization: A group of people who form a business, club, etc., together to achieve a particular aim.
- Change: The process of making somebody or something different.
- Profit: The money made in business or by selling things, especially after covering costs.
- Loss: The state of no longer having something or as much of something; the process that leads to this.
- Procedure: A way of doing something, especially the usual or correct way.
- Management: The activity of running and controlling a business or similar organization.
- Influence: The effect that somebody or something has on how a person thinks, behaves, or how something develops.
- Policy: A plan of action agreed upon or chosen by a political party, business, etc.

- Not-for-Profit: An organization that does not aim to make a profit.
- Profit-Making: A company or business that generates profit.
- Maximize: To increase something as much as possible.
- Minimize: To reduce something, especially something negative, to the lowest possible level.
- Government: The group of people responsible for controlling a country or state.
- Leadership: The state or position of being a leader.
- Goals: Something you hope to achieve.
- Employer: A person or company that pays people to work for them.
- Labour: Work, especially physical work.
- Investor: A person or organization that invests money in something.
- Palliative: A medicine or treatment that reduces pain without curing the cause.
- Inflation: A general rise in the prices of goods and services in a particular country, leading to a decrease in money value; the rate at which this occurs.
- Unemployment: The state of people not having a job; the number of people without employment.
- COVID-19: A disease caused by a coronavirus, first reported in 2019, which became a pandemic.
- Pandemic: A disease that spreads over an entire country or the world.
- Objective: Something you are trying to achieve.
- Customer: A person or organization that buys goods or services from a shop or business.
- Competition: An event in which people compete to determine who is the best at something.

- Loyalty: The quality of being consistently supportive of somebody or something.
- Client: A person who uses the services or advice of a professional or an organization.
- Effective: Producing the desired or intended result.
- Flexibility: The ability to adapt to new conditions or situations.
- Service: A system that provides something the public needs, organized by the government or a private company.
- Technology: Scientific knowledge applied in practical ways in industry, such as designing new machines.
- Education: The process of teaching, training, and learning, especially in schools, colleges, or universities, to improve knowledge and develop skills.
- Infrastructure: The fundamental systems and services necessary for a country or organization to function smoothly, such as buildings, transport, water, and power supplies.
- Deployment: The act of moving soldiers or weapons into a position for military action.
- Rule of Law: The condition in which all members of society, including political leaders, accept the authority of the law.
- Development: The steady growth of something so that it becomes more advanced or stronger.
- Commitment: A promise to do something, support someone, or behave in a particular way.
- Communication: The activity or process of expressing ideas and feelings or giving information.
- Teamwork: The activity of working well together as a team.

- Adaptation: The process of changing something to suit a new purpose or situation.
- Modification: The act or process of changing something to improve it or make it more acceptable.
- Poverty: The state of being poor.
- Income: The money earned by a person, region, or country from work, investments, or business activities.

Chapter 2| Review of Related Literature

2.1. Theoretical Framework

The Contingency Theory: The first theoretical framework for this study is the contingency theory of leadership. According to Samuel Certo and Trevis Certo (2006) in their book, "Modern Management," Fiedler's Contingency Theory of Leadership is predicated on the concept of leadership flexibility. This concept posits that successful leaders must change their leadership styles as they encounter different situations. This concept of leadership style flexibility is particularly apt in a recession. The Contingency Theory of leadership considers three key ingredients that should be evaluated when deploying leaders to function in situations that are appropriate for their leadership styles. These ingredients are:

- Leader-member relations: This is the degree to which a leader feels accepted by the followers.
- Task structure: This is the degree to which the goals, the work to be done, and other situational factors are clearly outlined.
- Position power: This is determined by the extent to which the leader has control over the rewards and punishments followers receive.
- These factors, as indicated in the table below, can be arranged in eight different combinations referred to as octants.

OCTANT	Leader-Member Relations	Task Structure	Leader Position Power
I	Good	High	Strong
II	Good	High	Weak
III	Good	Weak	Strong
IV	Good	Weak	Weak
V	Moderately poor	High	Strong
VI	Moderately poor	High	Weak
VII	Moderately poor	Weak	Strong
VIII	Moderately poor	Weak	Weak

Table 1: Eight Combinations or Octants of Three Factors

From the above table, leadership flexibility that combines the right mix of leader-member relations, task structure, and leader position has the potential to bring about organizational change during a recession.

The contingency leadership theory, otherwise known as situational theory, focuses on the context of a leader. These theories examine the situational effects on the success or failure of a leader. A leader's effectiveness is directly determined by the situational context. While a leader's personality is a small factor in their success, the most important factor is the context and situation in which they operate. This theory takes specific leadership styles and suggests that good leaders can adjust their leadership style according to the situation. It also suggests that it may be best to find the right kind of leader for a specific situation. Types of contingency theories include Hersey and Blanchard's Situational Theory, Evans and House's Path-Goal Theory, and Fiedler's Contingency Theory.

The contingency theory has significant advantages, including the ability of leaders to be effective regardless of their situational context. However, this theory has been criticized for not providing enough detail on the context of any given situation. While contingency theory focuses on the importance of a situation, it may not adequately consider the psychology of employees or the company itself. Additionally, it may not sufficiently address how leadership styles can evolve over time.

Both internal and external factors impact a leader and their situation. Internal factors include the type of company, the size of the team, and the innate leadership style of an individual. External factors may include customer perceptions and the marketplace. All these elements play a role in contingency theory.

Since leadership involves an individual taking center stage to influence followers, the personality traits, character, and behavior of the leader are critical to effective leadership. It is on this premise that examining trait and behavior theory becomes crucial.

The Trait Theory: A trait is a distinguishing quality or personal characteristic. The leadership trait theory focuses on the leader's values and beliefs, personality, need for achievement or acceptance, orientation to power, gender, confidence, and mental, physical, and emotional attributes. Decades ago, pioneers of leadership trait studies postulated that people were born with specific traits and that great leaders possessed peculiar (right) traits that made them effective. However, some researchers argue that there is a common trait among good and effective leaders.

Through extensive sociological and psychological studies between 1930 and 1950, researchers discovered a correlation between traits and leadership. A healthy personality trait in a leader will obviously result in healthy leadership. This is because, to a great extent, leadership stems from who we are. While there is currently no scientific way to measure personality traits, psychological research has established the existence of traits that can affect leadership positively or negatively, depending on where the leader falls on the continuum. However, leaders have the opportunity to learn and unlearn certain traits to become more effective. Since a leader's personality is the visible aspect of their character that influences others (followers), it plays a role in their capacity to lead effectively.

The Behavioral Theory: This leadership theory considers the observable actions and reactions of leaders and followers in a given situation. Researchers, faced with the challenge of measuring traits like confidence and loyalty, discovered a relationship between traits and behavior. According to researchers, behavior can be defined as a set of actions that embody a particular trait. Since behaviors are observable, measuring them is more scientifically valid than attempting to measure personality traits.

The behavioral theory differs from the trait theory. While the trait theory assumes that a leader is born with specific traits that make them a good leader, the behavioral theory assumes that leadership can be learned without relying entirely on inherent personality traits. Because leaders can choose their actions, and because actions define leadership, individuals can ultimately learn and choose to be good leaders.

Both trait and behavioral theories have limitations. However, leadership research has improved through two important behavioral studies conducted at the University of Michigan and Ohio State University. These studies identified two key behavioral categories—orientation toward tasks and orientation toward people.

The Michigan studies, which began in the late 1950s, identified three critical characteristics of effective leaders. First, they observed task-oriented behavior in managers who did not perform the same tasks as their subordinates. These managers spent time planning, coordinating, and overseeing task execution.

The second category of leaders exhibited relationship-oriented behavior. These managers focused on task execution but prioritized developing relationships with their subordinates. They provided support to their teams and emphasized both internal and external rewards. The third style of leadership was participative leadership, where the leader facilitated rather than directed. This leader worked to build a cohesive team to achieve collective results rather than focusing on individuals.

The Ohio State studies also examined leaders' orientation toward tasks versus people. These studies termed task-oriented behavior as 'initiating structure' and people-oriented behavior as 'consideration.'

There is an assumption that leaders are born, not made. This belief is based on the idea that some individuals possess innate qualities or abilities that make them natural leaders. To some extent, natural traits such as personality, emotional attributes, gender, and physical appearance may give a leader an advantage in certain environments. Many traditional communities have natural leaders who, despite lacking formal education, have successfully led their communities.

However, natural leadership can be improved through learning and development. While proponents of trait theory argue that some leaders are born with qualities that give them an edge, it is essential to recognize that leadership in a dynamic environment requires additional skills. The only option for natural leaders is to acquire new skills, research effective leadership practices, seek mentors, and ask questions. By doing so, they can enhance their leadership effectiveness and adapt to changing circumstances.

2.2. Conceptual Review

There are three concepts under review in this study: leadership, organizational change, and recession. While leadership and organizational change are independent variables, the concept of recession is a dependent variable.

2.2.1. Leadership

In their book *Modern Management*, Samuel C. Certo and S. Trevis Certo (2006) defined leadership as "the process of directing the behavior of others toward the accomplishment of some objective. Directing, in this sense, means causing individuals to act in a certain way or to follow a particular course. Ideally, this course is perfectly consistent with such factors as established organizational policies, procedures, and job descriptions. The central theme of leadership is getting things accomplished through people."

According to Ken Blanchard, "Leadership is influence." The U.S. Army defines leadership as influencing people by providing purpose, direction, and motivation while operating to accomplish the mission and improve the organization.

Five key variables have been identified in the concept of leadership, as indicated in the conceptual framework. These variables include:

- Influence
- Problem-solving ability
- Effective communication
- Commitment
- Emotional intelligence

2.2.3. Influence

According to Brian Solis (2010), influence is the ability to cause desirable and measurable actions and outcomes. He posits that the word *influence*, as well as the individuals referred to as *new influencers*, is elusive in terms of a standard definition. Defining influence is just the beginning. Understanding perception and expectations around influence and influencers helps us identify where we need to focus our time on education and innovation.

Merriam-Webster's Dictionary defines influence as "the power or capacity of causing an effect in indirect or intangible ways." It is the act or power of producing an effect without apparent exertion of force or direct exercise of command.

2.2.3. Problem-Solving Ability

Leadership entails solving real problems in organizations, particularly during a crisis. In an article published on the *Indeed Career Guide* website (2020), titled *Problem-Solving Skills: Definitions and Examples*, problem-solving ability is referred to as the ability to handle difficult or unexpected situations in the workplace, as well as complex business challenges. Organizations rely on people who can assess both types of situations and calmly identify solutions. Problem-solving skills are traits that enable leaders to do so. While problem-solving skills are valued by employers, they are also highly useful in other areas of life, such as relationship building and day-to-day decision-making.

Problem-solving skills help leaders determine the source of a problem and find efficient ways to propose effective solutions. While some authorities consider problem-solving an independent skill, it is important to note that several other related skills contribute to problem-solving ability. These include:

- Active listening
- Analysis
- Research
- Creativity
- Communication
- Dependability
- Decision-making

- Team-building

2.2.4. Effective Communication

In an article titled *The Role of Effective Communication in Strategic Management of Organizations*, published in the *International Journal of Humanities and Social Science*, the authors Lovelyn Okeowa and Kelvin Iloafu (2017) pointed out that communication is the art of passing information from one person to another so that it is received in the manner it was intended. There is a relationship between effective communication and the strategic management of organizations. Leaders can effect change in organizations to the extent that they are able to communicate effectively with team members and clients.

Leaders are expected to understand the nuances of effective communication. According to Ajoy Datta and Arnaldo Pellini (2011) in their work *Communicating Research: A Beginner's Guide for Researchers in Vietnam*, the following are important communication principles:

You can only communicate what you know.

Communication is a two-way process. The better you listen to your audience, the better you will be able to answer their needs, and the more your messages will be believed, liked, and ultimately acted upon.

Effective communicators know what their audience needs to know, what 'language' they understand, and what they look at and listen to.

You should develop tools that fit the channels available for your message.

You must develop messages that respect the cultural context of your audience.

You must understand and respect your communication abilities and limits, as well as your time and resources, as communication can be time- and skill-intensive work.

You must learn from your mistakes and successes to improve your future communications.

2.2.5. Commitment

Commitment is dedication to a particular organization, cause, or belief, along with a willingness to get involved. People who are committed to an organization or effort truly believe that it is important, and they show up, follow through, and remain dedicated.

According to Lorraine E. Anderson (2015) in her work *Relationship between Leadership, Organizational Commitment, and Intent to Stay among Junior Executives*, authentic leadership and integrity are key drivers of organizational commitment. The study suggested that there is a relationship between authentic leadership and affective organizational commitment, mediated through integrity.

In an article published in the June 2003 edition of *Harvard Business Review Magazine*, titled *Managing by Commitments*, the writer Donald Sull indicated that, despite differences in their personal attributes, successful managers all excel in making, honoring, and remaking commitments. Managerial commitments take many forms, from capital investments to hiring decisions to public statements, but each commitment exerts both immediate and enduring influence on a company. Over time and in combination, a leader's commitments shape a business's identity, define its strengths and weaknesses, establish its opportunities and limitations, and set its direction.

He added that commitments are extraordinarily powerful—a fact that executives can all too easily lose sight of.

In his thesis, "The Ingredients for a Committed Workforce," J.C. Drenth (2009) cited several authorities who have made academic contributions on the subject of commitment. He stated that, according to Meyer and Herscovitch, commitment is more than a state of mind that exists when an individual experiences a positive exchange in a relationship with some entity; it contributes to our understanding of organizational behavior (Meyer and Herscovitch, 2001).

He also stated that Bateman and Strasser (1984) believe that research focusing on commitment is crucial because of the following:

a. It affects employee behaviors. Frequent employee turnover in an organization, absenteeism, poor performance, and lack of motivation are, to some extent, related to a lack of commitment (Abelson & Sheridan, 1981; Angle & Perry, 1981; Bluedorn, 1982; Farrell & Rusbult, 1981; Marsh & Mannari, 1977; Morris & Sherman, 1981; Porter et al., 1976; Porter et al., 1974; Steers, 1977).
b. It affects attitudinal, affective, and cognitive constructs such as job involvement and job tension (Hall & Schneider, 1972; Hrebiniak & Alutto, 1972; Porter et al., 1974; Stevens, Beyer, & Trice, 1978; Stone & Porter, 1976).
c. It influences job tenure (Angle & Perry, 1981; Hall & Schneider, 1972; Hrebiniak & Alutto, 1972; Koch & Steers, 1978; Sheldon, 1971; Steers, 1977) (pp. 95-96).

According to Mowday (1998), there appears to be evidence linking specific human resource management systems with overall organizational performance and with affective commitment at the individual employee level. The linkage between human resource management strategies and individual-level employee commitment is also demonstrated by Tsui, Pearce, Porter, and Tripoli (1997). They found that organizational investment in employees (i.e., company-specific education) was associated with higher levels of employee affective commitment, as well as higher levels of citizenship behavior, greater intention to stay with the organization, and lower absenteeism. Because of this range of relationships, coupled with the belief that organizational commitment is a relatively stable attitude over time and is less seriously affected by transitory events, it is more strongly influenced by organizational factors such as leadership, culture, values, and norms when compared to job satisfaction (e.g., Porter et al., 1974; Mowday, Steers, & Porter, 1979; Matthieu & Kohler, 1990; Cohen, 1992; Sagie, 1993; Gellatly, 1995; Markham & McKee, 1995).

In the words of J.C. Drenth, commitment can be seen as a highly relevant management construct. Furthermore, findings indicate that commitment is often a better predictor of turnover than job satisfaction (Koch & Steers, 1976; Porter et al., 1974), which is also a frequently used construct. In fact, commitment may be the key source of competitive advantage, particularly in times of labor scarcity.

2.2.6. Emotional Intelligence

Emotional intelligence is a key variable in the concept of leadership, as indicated in this research work. The emotional intelligence skills of a leader play a significant role in restoring organizational stability during crises.

In a doctoral dissertation titled, "Emotional Intelligence and Leadership Effectiveness of Georgia's Technical College Department Chairs," the author, Mark Gibson Reddic (2007), cited Kouzes and Posner (2002), who posited that leaders must be socially competent at all levels and that "the skills of emotional intelligence are particularly central to leadership" (p. 264). He defined emotional intelligence as a form of intelligence that refers to the ability to recognize one's own feelings and the feelings of others, as well as the ability to motivate oneself and others. Furthermore, emotional intelligence is the ability to manage emotions well in oneself and in others, to differentiate among emotions, and to use this information to guide one's thinking and actions (Goleman, 2000b; Salovey & Mayer, 1990).

Kouzes and Posner further stated that, according to Daniel Goleman, "Interpersonal ineptitude in leaders lowers everyone's performance: it wastes time, creates acrimony, corrodes motivation and commitment, and builds hostility and apathy" (Kouzes & Posner, 2002, p. 264). Goleman, Boyatzis, and McKee (2002) stated:

> *Great leaders move us. They ignite our passion and inspire the best in us. When we try to explain why they are so effective, we speak of strategy, vision, or powerful ideas. But the reality is much more primal: Great leadership works through emotions* (p. 3).

According to Mark Gibson, Goleman, Boyatzis, and McKee (2001) compiled two years of new research suggesting that a leader's mood and behaviors actually determine the moods and behaviors of others in the organization. They stated that a leader's emotional intelligence creates a certain culture or work environment. Their research showed that higher levels of emotional intelligence created climates that encouraged information sharing, trust, healthy risk-taking, and learning. Conversely, lower levels of emotional intelligence created climates filled with fear and anxiety. To support their findings, Goleman et al. (2001) turned to the latest neurological and psychological research, referred to their work with business leaders, observed colleagues of hundreds of leaders, and analyzed data on the leadership styles of thousands of executives, including those in education.

> *From this body of research, we discovered that emotional intelligence is carried through an organization like electricity through wires. To be more specific, the leader's*

mood is quite literally contagious, spreading quickly and inexorably throughout the business (p. 44).

Goleman et al. (2001) indicated that if a leader's mood and accompanying behaviors are the cornerstones of business success, then a leader's primal task should be emotional leadership. A leader must ensure that, in addition to regularly being in an optimistic, authentic, high-energy mood, they also make sure that their followers feel and act that way too. *Managing for financial results, then, begins with the leader managing their inner life so that the right emotional and behavioral chain reaction occurs* (Goleman et al., 2001, p. 44). Goleman (2000b) asserted that the most effective leaders share one important trait: they all have a high degree of emotional intelligence. He stated that a high degree of emotional intelligence is a qualification for leadership. Others have said, "By now, most executives have accepted that emotional intelligence is as critical as IQ to an individual's effectiveness" (Druskat & Wolff, 2001, p. 81).

According to Goleman's (2000b) research, star performers "showed significantly greater strengths in a range of emotional competencies, among these influence, team leadership, political awareness, self-confidence, and achievement drive. On average, close to 90 percent of their success in leadership was attributable to emotional intelligence" (p. 34). Research has shown that leaders with high levels of emotional intelligence are more successful (Sosik & Megerian, 1999; George, 2000).

2.2.7. Organizational Change

The concept of organizational change is primarily a key consideration in this research work. Organizational change, as defined by Certo et al. (2006), is the process of modifying an existing organization to increase organizational efficiency, which is a measure of how an organization can achieve set objectives despite the obstacles posed in a recession. To make this concept of organizational change a reality, particularly during a recession, the leader must be courageous enough to swim against the tide by thinking outside the box and doing things that contradict the status quo. To lead successfully, the leader should consider strengthening organizational authority, allowing flexibility in role allocation to team members based on identified relevant skill sets needed in crisis moments. It is important to establish clear lines of effective communication among team members and employ modern technology. Depending on the organization's financial viability, some leaders may consider the option of downsizing human resources to cut overhead costs.

According to Tim Stobierski (2020), in an article published by Harvard Business School, "Organizational change refers to the actions in which a company or business alters a major component of its organization, such as its culture, the underlying technologies or infrastructure it uses to operate, or its internal processes. Organizational change management is the method of leveraging change to bring about a successful resolution, and it typically includes three major phases: preparation, implementation, and follow-through."

According to Tryggvi Hallgrimsson (2008) in his research work, "Organizational Change and Change Readiness: Employees' Attitude During Times of Proposed Merger," organizations need to take into consideration a multitude of different stakeholder expectations. Their own expectations and values need to be coherent with their prospective output. Also, organizations must take into account the wants and needs of society and the ideas society has regarding their functions and ultimate necessity. The ability of organizations to adapt and change has become a central research issue, focusing on the complexities of regulatory, political, technological, and social changes. So central, in fact, is change to the study of organizations that in an introduction to the *Handbook of Organizational Studies*, a book Dag Ingvar Jacobsen (2006, p. 13) calls a "bible" within organizational theory, the authors Clegg et al. explain: "...we did not include a chapter on change because we cannot imagine any theory of, or chapter on, organizations that is not about change" (1996, p. 11). Ten years later, when the book was published in a revised second edition, a chapter on radical organizational change was included, wherein authors Greenwood and Hinings (2006, p. 814) state that "[today, it is commonplace to note that the volatility of changes confronting organizations has dramatically increased." In light of competitive uncertainties, the notion of planning for the future is constantly changing.

Organizational change and the environmental turbulence of the modern market economy have brought about a need to redefine the meaning of career development (Adamson et al., 1998, pp. 253–256). Definitions of careers are changing. For employees in today's market economy, the importance of a "career for life" is becoming less significant. More important is their employability and the marketability of skills. Given an opportunity to advance within their occupation, stable work environments will ideally lead to job satisfaction and commitment to organizations (Curry, 2003, pp. 567–568). Stability, however, is seldom attainable within organizations for long periods. Employers are subject to both the changing demands of external environments and the resulting changing organizational structures implemented in response to these changes. In an effort to address organizations' need for clarity during times of change, the field of change management has been born. Organizational change has many faces and various manifestations, occurring due to societal or technical environmental changes, as well as being rooted within the socio-systemic structures of organizations themselves.

Change management is by no means a distinct discipline with clearly defined boundaries. Rather, it borrows from a number of disciplines, making the task of defining its core concepts much more difficult (e.g., Burnes, 2004b, p. 261; Burnes, 2005, p. 73). Multiple theories within the field of organizational change have attempted to address the complexities of modern organizations, but by some accounts, they have only produced "theoretical pluralism" (Van de Ven & Poole, 1995, p. 510). However, when stripping change processes to their bare essentials, the foundations of organizational change can be defined as taking place on three different levels: the individual level, the group level, and between and within the structural levels of the organizational system itself. Different types of organizational change can be broadly categorized as continuous or radical.

According to Tryggvi Hallgrimsson (2008), this categorization is used to distinguish between changes that occur over time in small proportions (continuous change) and changes that present a revolutionary divergence in operation and/or structure (radical change). It can be appropriately argued that no study of organization is able to overlook the importance of change. However, it is the extent of the changes that is often so hard to clarify, and the effects changes have on employees that are so hard to determine.

Hallgrimsson posits that if clichés carry truth, then truth lies in the cliché that modern society is moving at increasing speed. This is evident in the abundance of books on management that delineate the multiple effects of a "technological age" characterized by increasing competitiveness and the need for specialization. If society is moving fast, environments within it are also likely to be constantly changing. It is within this context of ever-changing environments that organizational change and, more specifically, change management has been established as a field within organizational studies. Organizations are sensitive to their environment and seek different ways to conduct operations. When the need for change is acknowledged, organizations consequently become subject to increased uncertainty. This is particularly evident when an organizational merger is part of the needed change (Tidd, 2001, p. 175).

In an article published in *Business News*, the writer stated that organizational change looks at both the process in which a company or any organization changes its operational methods, technologies, organizational structure, whole structure, or strategies, as well as the effects these changes have on it. Organizational change usually happens in response to—or as a result of—external or internal pressures.

It is all about reviewing and modifying structures—specifically management structures—and business processes.

Small commercial enterprises need to adapt to survive against larger competitors. They also need to learn to thrive in that environment. Large rivals need to adapt rapidly when a smaller, innovative competitor comes onto the scene.

To avoid falling behind or to remain a step ahead of its rivals, a business must seek out ways to operate more efficiently. It must also strive to operate more cost-effectively.

With the advent of the Internet, the business environment has undergone the process of change rather rapidly compared to a few decades ago. Organizational change is critical to the survival of any business or institution, particularly in a recession.

The concept of organizational change in the context of this study has some identifiable variables that need to be considered. These variables are innovation, creativity, adaptation, and modification.

2.2.8. Innovation

In an article titled *"Organizational Innovation and Organizational Change"*, published in the *Annual Review of Sociology*, J. T. Hage (1999) stated that although many lament the absence of cumulative findings in sociology, the study of organizational innovation is one instance where consistent findings have accumulated across more than thirty years of research. According to him, this was demonstrated in two recent reviews (Damanpour, 1991; Zammuto & O'Connor, 1992) published in the management literature. Innovation research, although previously not central to the concerns of many sociologists, now offers an opportunity to address a large number of important practical and theoretical issues.

In his submission, J. T. Hage stated that, from a practical point of view, since a country's economic development depends largely on the continuous launch of new products, governments have become increasingly concerned about innovation. Indeed, new products and services provide employment opportunities and positive trade balances, thus protecting the nation's standard of living. However, innovation in products, services, technologies, and administrative practices is also relevant to other institutional sectors besides the economy. The study of organizational innovation, for instance, aligns with research on significant breakthroughs in science, the development of superior military equipment, the creation of interdisciplinary programs in higher education (Blau, 1973), and welfare reforms. In other words, for anyone interested in some of the most fundamental societal issues, the subject of organizational innovation is highly relevant.

The author further emphasized that, from a theoretical perspective, research on organizational innovation opens new avenues for exploring several emerging issues, including societal evolution and institutional change, the dynamics of knowledge societies (Bell, 1973; Hage & Powers, 1992), and the integration of macro- and micro-level analyses. Beyond sociology, organizational innovation contributes to key areas of economic research. The most obvious application is in national systems of innovation (Lundvall, 1992; Nelson, 1993), but it is equally relevant to endogenous theories of economic growth (Romer, 1986, 1990; Solow, 1992).

Businesses have recognized the importance of innovation for survival in a globally competitive environment. A recent report from the British Department of Trade and Industry (Sullivan, 1998) indicates that major companies—regardless of country (France, Germany, Italy, Japan, Sweden, the United Kingdom, and the United States)—allocate between 4% and 5% of their sales revenue to research in the automobile and commercial aircraft industries, between 5% and 8% in semiconductor, computer, electrical, and chemical product sectors, and between 10% and 15% in the health products, pharmaceuticals, and software sectors. In the past year, research and development (R&D) spending among the top

300 companies worldwide increased by 12.8%, with the largest increases seen in about 100 American companies. While this may be an exceptional surge, it continues the long-term trend since 1975 (Hage & Powers, 1992:32), with an annual growth rate of 4% to 5% above inflation in private expenditure, at least among American firms.

According to Hiner (2007) in his work *Innovation Leadership: A Dissertation Monograph*, innovation has a variety of definitions, depending on the perspective of the person defining it. For instance, someone in the Research and Development (R&D) department of an electronics manufacturer might view innovation as the creative process required to respond to customer needs with new product ideas. In contrast, someone in the banking industry might define innovation as a new process that enables customers to transact business more efficiently, saving operational costs or generating additional revenue.

According to the author, in the glossary of his definitive work on innovation, *Diffusion of Innovations* (Rogers, 2003), Everett Rogers defines innovation as "an idea, practice, or object that is perceived as new by an individual or other unit of adoption" (p. 475). This definition frames innovation from the perspective of its adoption—it is whatever is perceived as new by the adopter. However, it also introduces universal innovation concepts such as *idea, practice, or object*, novelty, and adoption. While "practice" and "object" are commonly associated with the services and products generated by innovative companies, the idea that an *idea* itself can be an innovation is somewhat unconventional in modern usage. Nevertheless, Rogers began his investigations into innovation adoption in the 1960s as a sociological study; he sought to understand how new ideas spread across novice populations. The notion that innovation is strictly a technological breakthrough is a more recent development. Robert

Burgelman and Leonard Sayles (Burgelman & Sayles, 1986) define innovation as "a company's efforts in instituting new methods of production and/or bringing new products or services to market" (p. 10), reinforcing the prevailing notion that an idea must be realized in some tangible way to be considered an innovation.

Some authors further categorize innovation as either incremental (also called sustaining) or disruptive (Christensen, 2003; Christensen & Raynor, 2003; Moore, 2005). An incremental innovation advances an existing product or service by enhancing its functionality without altering its fundamental structure, function, or purpose. As Christensen observes, "What all sustaining technologies have in common is that they improve the performance of established products along the dimensions that mainstream customers in major markets have historically valued" (p. xviii). For example, upgrading software from version 1.0 to 2.0 is an incremental innovation—it retains the basic function of the software while introducing new features and fixing previous inadequacies.

Conversely, a disruptive innovation displaces existing technology or discovers an entirely new market niche, either addressing current market needs or creating new ones. Moore (2005) states, "This type of innovation creates new market categories based on a discontinuous technology change or a disruptive business model." An example of a disruptive innovation is the cellular telephone, which has largely replaced payphones and, to some extent, mobile radios (e.g., citizens band, amateur, and professional radios) as a means of voice communication between individuals. Initially, disruptive technologies typically underperform in the market, but they eventually surpass the existing technology they replace.

Lawrence Hiner suggests that in order for an idea to transition from market observation to a tangible product or service, innovation progresses through various stages:

- Ideation: The generation of new product or service ideas. At this stage, novelty and uniqueness are key aspects.
- Invention: The realization of creative ideas in their earliest prototypical forms.
- Instantiation: The process of constructing and prototyping the innovation. At this stage, the innovation moves toward commercial realization and is refined based on market demands.
- Adoption: The acceptance of the innovation by targeted users. This stage is often considered essential for commercial success (Davila, Epstein, & Shelton, 2006); without adoption, "good ideas" never mature into true "innovations."

2.2.9. Creativity

Rothenberg and Hausman highlight a historical background to creativity, referring to Plato, Aristotle, Kant, Galton, and Freud, who, in their various epochs, influenced the history of creativity (1976, pp. 31-48). [1]Plato saw creative activity as a gift of divine inspiration, not subject to rational analysis. He describes 'inspiration' as a catalyzing factor in creative behavior—a way to generate alternatives (within a 'supernaturalist' context)—while Aristotle distinguishes between two kinds of reason: the one we use when we think about the changing world (a calculable reason) and another by which we contemplate the eternal (scientific knowledge). Ultimately, he embraces some aspects of natural laws but not as deriving merely by 'chance' (Aristotle, 1999a[2]; Gardner, 1988)[3]. Immanuel Kant, on his part, identifies that creative actions are directly dependent on 'spontaneous activity' through the conscious mind (Antonites, 2003)[4].

Francis Galton (1822-1911), an exponent of the hereditary school of creativity (best known for his pioneering work on human intelligence), considers creativity as the result of prepotency and uses the term 'genius' in line with the creative person, characteristic of a non-average individual. He argues that both contain talent qualities that flow from generation to generation and are thus inherited (Crovitz, 1970[5]; Gardner, 1988).

Sigmund Freud, the father of psychoanalysis, on his part, argues that the phenomenon of creativity contains finite 'dynamic factors' in the human mind, with creative efforts as a consequence. Drawing insights from analyzing writers and comparing them with children playing, he concludes that both create an imaginative world that forms part of creative thinking and action (Antonites, 2003).

Be that as it may, contemporary studies on creativity stress the confluence of different classical theories. For example, the confluence theory suggests that creativity consists of multiple dimensions comprising cognitive, personality, and social traits (Antonites, 2003).

2.2.10. Emergence of Research on Creativity

Creativity has been linked to genius in the sciences, business, and art, and quite a number of individuals have attained heroic status through their creative philosophies, discoveries, practices, and products (Puccio[6], 1991; Eysenck[7], 2008). As such, in addition to being a personality trait, creativity is grounded in both sociology and psychology, thereby acknowledging its subjective rather than objective leaning. Though numerous attempts have been made at modeling, measuring, and testing creativity, it is recognized that no single interpretation has been able to capture its essence.

Creativity is also viewed as a central element in problem-solving and decision-making and can result in profitable outcomes (Fillis[8], 2006; Fillis and Rentschler[9], 2010).

To this end, research explorations into notions of creativity and entrepreneurship have often originated from different worldviews and disciplines, such as psychology (Guilford[10], 1951; Sternberg, 2006a[11], 2006b[12]) and economics. Explorations into creativity were largely stimulated by calls in that direction from American psychologist Joy Paul Guilford to the American Psychological Association in 1950. He raised concerns about the paucity or near-total absence of research into creativity, following which there was a widespread increase in the number of journals devoted to creativity explorations (Roweton, 1989; Kabanoff and Bottger, 2001; Lubart, 2000; Amabile, 1996; Unsworth, 2001).

For Sternberg (a renowned psychometrist and author of over a thousand books and articles on creativity and related concepts), there are five commonalities in creativity explorations around the world:

a. First, creativity "involves thinking that aims at producing ideas or products that are relatively novel and, in some respects, compelling."
b. Second, creativity has both domain-specific and domain-general elements. That is to say, it requires specific knowledge, but certain elements of creativity cut across different domains.
c. Third, creativity is measurable, at least to some extent.
d. Fourth, it can be developed and promoted.
e. Fifth, "creativity is not highly rewarded in practice" (Sternberg, 2006a).

2.2.11. Nature and Scope of Creativity

Creativity is influenced by thinking styles, motivation, and culture, and each individual is born with domain-specific abilities. For example, some people are more talented in art or music than others. In other words, some believe that creativity is an inherent or inherited characteristic that only some lucky people are born with, while others believe that creativity occurs accidentally following unpremeditated events or necessity, leading to the aphorism, "necessity is the mother of invention." Others assume it is a process that can be taught and facilitated irrespective of inherited or natural traits an individual may possess (Sternberg & O'Hara, 1999; Amabile, 1983; Fillis & Rentschler, 2010).

Edward De Bono, author of more than 60 books in 40 languages, recaps the myths of creativity as comprising:

a) Creativity is an innate skill and cannot be acquired through training.
b) You need to be a rebel to be seen as creative.
c) Artists are the only creative beings. d. You need to be 'crazy' before creativity will kick in. e. Intelligence and creativity; all new products were accidental discoveries (De Bono, 1996).

However, in contrast to the historic 'lone genius' notions of creativity, the trait is now understood both as a potential of every individual and as involving the active construction of new ideas and content within social contexts (Truman, 2011). To this end, West (1997) highlights that creativity is not limited to a chosen few but is a fundamental part of being human, given that it involves bringing together knowledge from different areas of experience to produce new and improved ideas, all of which are naturally inclined within all humans, though to varying degrees.

Helson (1996) adds that there is no unitary personality profile typical of highly creative people that distinguishes them from the less creative. Eysenck (1997), however, identifies autonomy, nonconformity, openness to stimuli, flexibility, tolerance of ambiguity, inner-directedness, and ego strength, among others, as favorable traits for creativity.

Be that as it may, a widely accepted position is that creativity is based on intrinsic motivation— the desire to carry out an activity for the sake of the activity itself. This may be contrasted with working for external rewards or avoiding punishment (extrinsic motivation) (Amabile, 1996; Cropley & Urban, 2000).

Treffinger, Sortore, and Cross highlight the importance of what they call the "full 'ecological system' of creativity," which involves recognizing creativity's interaction with other psychological properties of the individual, aspects of the creative process, effects of the situation, characteristics of the task itself, and the nature of the desired product (1993, p. 560).

Cropley and Urban (2000) suggest that, with reference to the social environment, creativity requires:

a. Acceptance of differences
b. Openness and tolerance to variability
c. Renunciation of rigid sanctions against harmless mistakes d. Provision of a 'creativogenic' climate

According to Sternberg and Lubart (1991, 1992, 1995, 1996), creative individuals, by their nature, tend to defy the crowd. They resist merely thinking or doing what others are thinking or doing. Rather, they go off in their own direction, seeking to propose ideas that are both novel and useful in some way.

The greatest obstacle to creativity, however, is not merely external restrictions but the limitations one places on one's own thinking. Such limitations, however, may derive from processes of enculturation and socialization, making it unclear whether restrictions on creativity are internally or externally imposed (Sternberg & Lubart, 1991, 1992, 1995).

Sternberg's 'investment theory of creativity,' proposed in collaboration with Todd Lubart, holds that creativity is, in large part, a decision. Specifically, it is a decision to buy low and sell high in the world of ideas. Creativity is a decision in the same way investing is. People are not born creative or uncreative; rather, they develop a set of attitudes toward life that characterize those who are willing to go their own way. Examples of such attitudes include the willingness to:

a. Redefine problems in novel ways
b. Take sensible risks
c. 'Sell' ideas that others might not initially accept
d. Persevere in the face of obstacles
e. Examine whether their own preconceptions interfere with their creative process

Such attitudes are teachable and can be ingrained in students through instruction that encourages them to think for themselves (Sternberg & Lubart, 1991, 1992).

2.2.12. Defining Creativity

Findlay and Lumsden (1988, p. 9) define the creative person as someone with the ability to solve a problem in a situation where the context of the problem and interpretation is unclear. Boden (1994, p. 75) adds that this creative individual generates new ideas out of existing concepts, resulting in outcomes that are typically 'interesting.'

Cropley and Urban distinguish 'thinking' as the use of existing information to produce further information. With reference to the problem-solving character of 'creativity,' they suggest that it involves analyzing the particular form of a problem, selecting from among the masses of information available at any moment, relating new information to what is already known, combining elements of new and old

information, evaluating newly emerging combinations, selectively retaining successful combinations, and communicating the results to others (Cropley & Urban, 2000). This definition aligns with that of Torrance, cited in Jalan and Kleiner (1995), who describe creativity as:
a process of being sensitive to problems, deficiencies, gaps in knowledge, missing elements, disharmonies, and so on; identifying difficulty; searching for solutions; making guesses or formulating hypotheses about the deficiencies; testing and retesting them; and finally communicating the results.

Torrance (1994, p. 7) further states that some degree of creativity occurs whenever people solve problems for which they previously had no learned solution. Creativity is the process of sensing problems or gaps in information, forming ideas or hypotheses, testing and modifying these hypotheses, and communicating the results.

De Bono (1992, 1995, p.16) defines creativity as the formulation or creation of something that was not previously available in its present state. Value is continually placed on or added to the new creation. This is compared to the work of an artist who is always creating something new, which consequently has a certain value. As such, creativity concerns changes in perceptions and concepts and deals with the generation of alternatives and ideas that can be used in the problem-solving process.
For Lubart (1994), creativity is the capacity to produce novel or original work that fits within task constraints. Similarly, Ward, Finke, and Smith (1995) argue that it is the development of appropriate and novel solutions.

Again, creativity involves forming multiple perspectives of a situation (Guilford, 1967; Runco, 1996), implying, therefore, that creative ideas are inspired by previous situations and experiences.

Majaro (1988) holds that creativity is the thinking process that results in the development and generation of new ideas, while innovation is the practical application of the concept to achieve set goals on a commercial or profit basis.

Feldman, Csikszentmihalyi, and Gardner (1994, p.1), on their part, define creativity as the achievement of something remarkable and new—something that transforms and changes a field of endeavor in a significant way.

For Amabile (1983), creativity is an ability and also a mental activity. It takes place in conditions that either facilitate or inhibit it. Its product is creative outcomes. It is a sudden insight, a leap ahead, or a spark, all of which emphasize discontinuity from a past state.

For Brazeal and Herbert (1999, p.35), creativity is the process through which invention occurs. This means that creativity is the enabling process by which something new comes into existence.

2.2.12. Characteristics of Creativity

Creativity is chiefly about person, process, product, press (situation), persuasion, and potential (Runco, 2007, p.384). However, Sternberg's "investment theory of creativity" describes creativity as a confluence of six distinct but interrelated resources: intellectual abilities, knowledge, styles of thinking, personality, motivation (especially intrinsic motivation), and environment (Sternberg, 2006b).

Sternberg (2006b) further suggests that the intellectual skills required for creativity include three particular skills:

- Synthetic skill – the ability to see problems in a new way and to escape the bounds of conventional thinking.
- Analytical skill – the ability to recognize which of one's ideas are worth pursuing.

- Practical-contextual skill – the ability to persuade others of the value of one's ideas.

A person may have the ability to be creative but lack the willingness to take sensible risks. At the same time, an individual may have a creative attitude but, without the skills of creativity (such as reconciling opposing ideas and engaging in dialectical thinking), may not reach his or her full creative potential. It is, therefore, crucially important, especially in schools, to provide an environment that allows creativity to flourish—not just in word, but also in deed (Sternberg & Lubart, 1991, 1992).

Houtz and Krug (1995) provide a review of several tests developed for assessing creativity within the category of divergent thinking. These include:

- The *Torrance Test of Creative Thinking* (TTCT) (Torrance, 1966, 1974, 1984, 1990, 1998)
- *Wallach and Kogan Tests* (1965)
- The *Guilford Battery* (Guilford, 1962, 1971)
- However, they highlight that the most widely used of these is the TTCT.

McFadzean (2000, p.15) recaps the traits of a creative person as follows:

a. A desire to achieve a goal or a winning attitude.
b. A high level of motivation, dedication, and commitment.
c. A high level of self-confidence, a willingness to take risks, and an acceptance of failure.
d. The ability to link different (unrelated) elements or entities.
e. The ability to assimilate negativity regarding failed projects or attempts.
f. The ability to shift existing paradigms and assess different perspectives.
g. The capacity to conceptualize problems and opportunities in a new or different way.

h. A "single-minded" vision or roadmap.
i. A working style that balances hard work and relaxation to enhance incubation.
j. The ability to determine whether creativity should take place individually or in a group.
Other traits include persistence, self-confidence, independence, an attraction to complexity, tolerance of ambiguity, intuitiveness, a love for work, and a propensity for risk-taking

2.2.13. Adaptation

In an article published in the *Journal of Management*, the authors Andrew Sarta et al. (2020) presented their view on organizational adaptation. In their view, organizational adaptation is equivocal. On the one hand, the concept is ubiquitous in management research and acts as the glue binding together the central issues of organizational change, performance, and survival. On the other hand, it lurks around in various guises (e.g., "fit," "alignment," "congruence," and "strategic change"), studied from multiple theoretical streams (e.g., behavioral, resource-based, and institutional) and at different levels of analysis (e.g., organization and industry levels). According to the authors, they used a novel approach to reviewing 443 adaptation articles that leveraged both computational and hand-coded analysis to produce an interactive visual of the themes most studied by adaptation scholars. They were able to inductively draw out a definition of adaptation as intentional decision-making undertaken by organizational members, leading to observable actions that aim to reduce the distance between an organization and its economic and institutional environments. The authors reviewed the literature across three main areas of inquiry and six theoretical perspectives that surfaced from their analysis and identified 11 difficulties that have hampered adaptation research in the past 50 years. Their review suggested ways to address these difficulties to enable future research to develop and accumulate.

Andrew Sarta et al. (2020) opined that adaptation is perhaps one of the most pervasive concepts in organizational theory and strategic management. They cited other authorities, including Chakravarthy (1982: 35), who described adaptation as "the primary purpose of strategic management." Dating back to the early 20th century and the emergence of scientific management (Taylor, 1911) and industrial administration (Fayol, 1916, 1949), multiple perspectives have underscored the role of adaptation in explaining organizational success (Aldrich & Ruef, 2006). Underlying much of the literature is the assumption that managers possess the capacity to assess their environments and capitalize on relevant opportunities to act, be successful, and increase their organizations' survival odds.

Unfortunately, the broad applicability of adaptation has led to the proliferation of imperfect synonyms (e.g., "fit," "alignment," "congruence") that are applied in place of or alongside adaptation, blurring comprehension of the notion. From the 1980s onward, discrepant voices objected to the view of an all-adaptive organizational capacity and brought forth the selective forces of economic environments (Aldrich, 1979; Hannan & Freeman, 1989; McKelvey, 1982). Complicating matters further, adaptation contains a potent analogy with biology, which does not easily translate to the field of management (Durand, 2006; Hodgson, 2013; Vergne & Depeyre, 2016). As a result, organizational scholars have used the concept of adaptation inconsistently across research traditions (e.g., behavioral theory, population ecology, neoinstitutionalism) without always being able to push the research agenda beyond analogical reasoning (e.g., much like a living organism, when an organization changes something and survives, it looks "as if" it has adapted to its environment).

According to these authors, adaptation has been reviewed both in general overviews of the environment–organization interface (Aldrich, 1979; Aldrich & Ruef, 2006; Durand, 2006) and in specific contexts (Eggers & Park, 2018). These studies debate how organizational adaptation relates to other concepts while eschewing scrutiny of the concept of adaptation itself, potentially contributing to the ambiguities identified at the outset. To use Kipling's metaphor, they observe one aspect of the elephant without considering the whole animal. A specific review of adaptation can harness the merits of past research, define the concept of adaptation more precisely to make the proverbial elephant whole again, identify existing difficulties in the literature, and delineate solutions to address those difficulties.

To ground their review, the authors first leveraged the approach of Podsakoff, MacKenzie, and Podsakoff (2016) and inductively drew out a definition of organizational adaptation as intentional decision-making undertaken by organizational members, leading to observable actions that aim to reduce the distance between an organization and its economic and institutional environments. According to the authors, a boundary condition for this review is a focus on established organizations as opposed to new ventures, since the latter, by definition, do not yet have a legacy resource base in need of adjustment vis-à-vis external environments.

Their definition distinguishes adaptation from generic strategic change and refocuses adaptation research around a specific type of intentional change aimed at increasing convergence between the organization and (some of) its environment(s). Armed with this definition, the authors were better equipped to distinguish adaptation from its triggers (e.g., pursuing change, responding to institutional pressure) and consequences (e.g., performance, survival). Their review clarifies that not every change is necessarily adaptive and that not every adaptive move necessarily increases organizational performance. Their review guides scholars toward consistent uses of adaptation that can resolve ambiguities and promote new insights for both disciplinary and interdisciplinary research (McMahan & Evans, 2018).

The authors averred that the conceptual roots of adaptation emanate from a natural integration of organizational theory and strategic management, most prominently in the work of Chandler (1962), which layered the ideas of strategic decision-making and functional efficiency onto the concept of adaptation. Classical works, such as *A Behavioral Theory of the Firm* (Cyert & March, 1963) and *Differentiation and Integration in Complex Organizations* (Lawrence & Lorsch, 1967), influenced and explicitly elaborated on the related notions of "adaptation" and "fit." Cyert and March (1963) identified the adaptation of decision rules as a critical element in the learning process, whereby organizations evaluate feedback received from the environment and attempt to reconcile misalignments. Concurrently, Lawrence and Lorsch (1967) elaborated on the strategy–structure relationship by identifying the optimal configurations of differentiation and integration that catalyzed research in structural contingency theory. The appropriate fit between internal structures and external sub-environments facilitated superior performance for organizations (Lawrence & Lorsch, 1967).

The authors stated that both seminal works established an association between adaptation and fit as notions describing the interface between organizations and environments. Moreover, *Merriam-Webster* (n.d.) explicitly relates these two terms by defining "adaptation" as the noun form of the verb "adapt," which means "to make fit (as for a new use) often by modification." Yet, nuanced interpretations of what it means to adapt developed over time, with prominent works emphasizing different aspects of fit, fitness, ability, and modification to varying degrees (Chakravarthy, 1982; Hrebiniak & Joyce, 1985; Levinthal, 1997; Miles, Snow, Meyer, & Coleman, 1978; Starbuck, 1971).

a. Citing Podsakoff et al. (2016), and in order to align around a common definition, the authors extracted and summarized the core aspects of adaptation from definitions provided in 18 seminal works from the 1940s to the early 2000s. More specifically, their definition conceptualizes adaptation as:
b. Intentional, meaning it is rooted in organizational members' awareness of their environment, resulting in a choice to react to, anticipate, or ignore changes in the environment.
c. Relational, whereby organizations and environments influence one another.
d. Conditioned, since environmental characteristics also depend on, and evolve with, other organizations' actions.
e. Convergent, in that organizations seeking to adapt attempt to move closer to a set of environmental characteristics.

2.2.14. Modification

In an article on Organizational Behavior shared by Khushboo Sinha, it is observed that the concept of Behavior Modification, or OB MOD, is derived from and developed based on the work of B.F. Skinner. It is a technique that helps managers and leaders modify or eliminate undesirable behavior and replace it with behavior that aligns with goal attainment. Behavior modification, therefore, is a technique for adjusting the behavior of organizational members or existing organizational structures to enhance organizational efficiency.

In a publication on behavior modification by OpenStax.org (2020), the authors opined that behavior modification is the use of operant conditioning principles to shape human behavior to conform to desired standards defined by superiors. In recent years, according to the authors, behavior modification has been applied in a wide variety of organizations. In most cases, positive results have been reported. There is growing interest in the technique as a management tool to improve performance and reduce costs.
The authors believe that, due to its emphasis on shaping behavior, it is more appropriate to think of behavior modification as a technique for motivating employees rather than as a theory of work motivation. It does not attempt to provide a comprehensive model of the various personal and job-related variables that contribute to motivation. Instead, its managerial focus is on how to motivate, which is likely the reason for its current popularity among some managers. The authors caution against the unquestioned acceptance of any technique without fully understanding the assumptions underlying the model. If the underlying assumptions of a model appear uncertain or inappropriate in a particular situation or organization, its use should be reconsidered.

To illustrate behavior modification in organizations, the authors cited the example of Japan's "Hell Camp." According to them, there is a saying in Japan: "The nail that sticks up gets hammered down." This implies that in corporate Japan, employees are expected to act together and move in unison, with individuality being discouraged. Japanese companies employ various techniques to train their employees to work hard and overcome adversity as a group. One particularly notable approach is known as Hell Camp. The concept behind Hell Camp is behavior modification. According to the publication, the purpose of Hell Camp is to train employees to "concentrate under difficulty." Representing a blend of

Outward Bound and assertiveness training, Hell Camp is designed to toughen employees by subjecting them to numerous humiliating exercises (e.g., making them shout their company song outside the local train station). If they complete each exercise successfully (for instance, if they shout loudly enough and with sufficient emotion), they are allowed to remove one of several "badges of shame." The criteria for removing a badge are deliberately vague. Essentially, the program employs a variable-ratio reinforcement system, meaning the employee never knows exactly when the trainer will declare success. As a result, the most likely level of performance that will lead to the removal of shame badges is at the higher end of the performance spectrum. If the employee succeeds in removing all badges during the week-long program and demonstrates sincerity and commitment, they graduate. If not, they must repeat the program.

2.2.14.1. Assumptions of Behavior Modification

The foundation of behavior modification as a management technique rests on three key ideas.

First, advocates of behavior modification believe that individuals are essentially passive and reactive rather than proactive. They tend to respond to stimuli in their environment rather than taking personal responsibility for initiating behavior. This assertion contrasts with cognitive theories of motivation (such as expectancy/valence theory), which argue that individuals make conscious decisions about their present and future behaviors and take an active role in shaping their environment.

Second, behavior modification focuses on observable and measurable behavior rather than unobservable needs, attitudes, goals, or motivational levels. In contrast, cognitive theories consider both observable and unobservable factors related to motivation. Social learning theory, in particular, argues that individuals can change their behavior simply by observing others and noticing the punishments or rewards associated with the observed behaviors.

Third, behavior modification emphasizes that permanent behavioral changes occur only through reinforcement. Behaviors that are positively reinforced will be repeated (i.e., learned), whereas behaviors that are not reinforced will diminish, in accordance with the law of effect.

2.2.14.2. Designing a Behavior Modification Program

For behavior modification techniques to be effective, their application must be well-designed and systematically implemented. Systematic attempts to introduce these programs typically go through five phases.

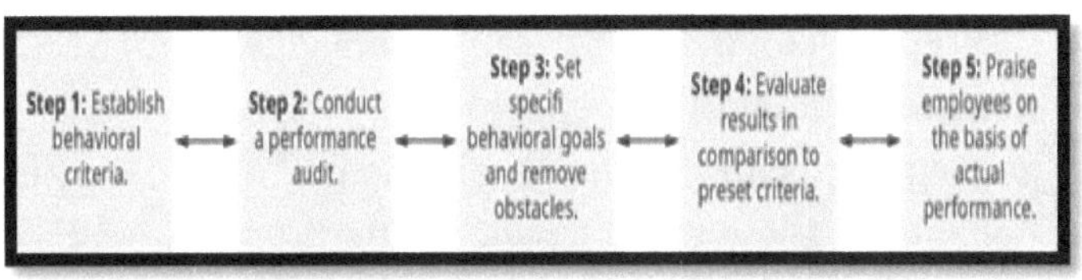

Exhibit 4.8 Steps in Implementing a Behavior

- Modification Program (Attribution: Copyright Rice University, OpenStax, under CC BY-NC-SA 4.0 license)
- Establishing Clear Behavioral Criteria. First, management attempts to define and clearly specify the behavioral aspects of acceptable performance. Management must be able to designate what constitutes acceptable behavior in terms that employees can understand, and this specification must be in objective, measurable terms. Examples of behavioral criteria include good attendance, promptness in arriving for work, and completing tasks on schedule. Sometimes, it is difficult to determine

suitable objective indicators of successful performance. For instance, as a training director of a major airline asked, "How do you quantify what a flight attendant does?" Even so, there are many situations and work behaviors that lend themselves to clear specification.

- Conducting a Performance Audit. Once acceptable behavioral criteria have been specified, a performance audit can be conducted. Because management is concerned about the extent to which employees are successfully meeting the behavioral criteria, the audit aims to pinpoint trouble spots where desired behaviors are not being carried out. For instance, a review of attendance records in various departments may reveal a department where absenteeism or tardiness is unusually high. Action can then be taken to focus on the problem area. In short, the performance audit aims to identify discrepancies between what management sees as desired or acceptable behavior and actual behavior.
- Setting Specific Behavioral Goals: Third, specific behavioral goals must be set for each employee. Failure to specify concrete behavioral goals is a primary reason for the failure of many behavior modification programs. Examples of such goals include decreasing absenteeism or tardiness, reducing product defects on an assembly line, and meeting production schedules. The goals should be both realistic (that is, reasonably achievable by the employees) and acceptable to them. Otherwise, the goals lack relevance, and the resulting effort will diminish.
- Evaluating Results: Next, employees and supervisors keep track of the employee's performance record compared to the preset behavioral criteria and goals. Discrepancies are noted and discussed. For example, the record could provide employees with continuous

feedback on the extent to which they are on target in meeting their defect reduction goals.

- Administering Feedback and Rewards: Finally, based on the assessment of the employee's performance record, the supervisor administers feedback and, where warranted, praise. For example, praise could strengthen the employees' efforts to reduce defects (positive reinforcement). The withholding of praise for defect levels deemed less than adequate or below established goals could cause employees to stop behaviors contributing to defects or work harder to reduce defects (extinction).
- Central to this phase of the process is the notion of shaping. Shaping is the process of improving performance incrementally, step by step. Suppose an employee is absent 30 percent of the time during one month. To improve attendance, a goal is set to reduce absenteeism to only 5 percent. After implementing the above procedure, absenteeism falls to 20 percent in the second month. Although this is not at goal level, it is clearly an improvement and, as such, is rewarded. The next month, absenteeism falls to 15 percent, and again, the incremental improvement is rewarded. Hence, through this incremental approach, the employee gets ever closer to the desired level of behavior. In other words, we have "shaped" her behavior.

2.2.14.3. Behavior Modification in Practice

The authors opined that there are many ways to see how the principles of behavior modification can be applied in organizational settings. Perhaps one of the best examples can be found in a classic study carried out by Luthans and Kreitner. These researchers conducted a field experiment in a medium-sized light manufacturing plant. Two separate groups of supervisors were used in the study.

In one group, the supervisors were trained in the techniques of behavior modification. This program was called 10 weeks on behavioral change strategies. The second group of supervisors (the control group) received no such training. Afterward, the trained supervisors were asked to implement what they had learned among their groups; obviously, the control group supervisors were given no such instructions.

After 10 weeks, group performance was examined for all groups. Two types of data were collected. First, the researchers were interested in possible behavioral changes among the various workers in the experimental groups (compared to the control groups) as a result of the behavior modification efforts. Significantly, the following changes were noted in areas targeted for change:

- The frequency of complaints among group members declined.
- Scrap rates declined.
- Group quality indicators increased.
- The frequency of individual performance problems declined.
- No such changes were recorded for the control groups not exposed to behavior modification.

The second measure taken focused on the overall performance rates for the various groups. This was calculated as a measure of direct labor effectiveness for each group. Again, overall group performance—that is, labor effectiveness ratings—improved significantly in the experimental groups but remained unchanged in the control groups. The researchers concluded that the introduction of the behavior modification program led to substantive improvements in factory performance.

2.2.14.4. Recession

According to Tejvan Pettinger (2020), in his article *Impact of Economic Recession*,

"A recession (fall in national income) will typically be characterized by high unemployment, falling average incomes, increased inequality, and higher government borrowing. The impact of a recession depends on how long it lasts and the depth of the fall in output."

1. He enumerated the main costs of a recession as follows:
2. Unemployment
3. Fall in income – shorter working weeks
4. Rise in poverty
5. Fall in asset prices (e.g., house prices, stock market)
6. Increased inequality and an increase in relative poverty
7. Higher government borrowing (less tax revenue)
8. Permanently lost output
9. Firms going out of business

The worst affected will be those who lose their jobs or see their hours/self-employed income dramatically fall.

The impact also depends on the type of recession. The 2009 recession hit the financial sector the hardest. Many highly paid "white-collar" workers lost their jobs. Banks saw large-scale losses and declining profits. It also severely affected the housing sector.

The 2020 recession was different. It particularly affected low-income workers in the leisure and tourism sectors, which were devastated by the Coronavirus pandemic. The effect also depended on whether a worker could work from home (e.g., a writer) or had a job in the physical economy, which suffered more (e.g., selling coffee). Additionally, the impact varied based on the extent of government support and whether people were entitled to benefits or rent relief.

2.2.14.5. Unemployment

According to information from www.economicshelp.org (2019), a fall in economic output will cause a rise in unemployment. This is because:

- Some firms will go bankrupt, meaning workers will lose their jobs.
- Firms will lay off workers to try and reduce costs.
- Firms will cut back on hiring new workers.

In the 2009 recession, unemployment in the UK rose to over 2.6 million. However, given the depth of the recession, one might have expected it to be even higher (e.g., in the 1980s, unemployment rose to over 3 million). In contrast, many European countries experienced a catastrophic rise in unemployment, with rates exceeding 20% in countries such as Greece, Spain, and Portugal.

Unemployment figures may underestimate the true level of unemployment. For example, during a recession, the self-employed may experience a dramatic fall in income but may not be classified as unemployed. During the Great Depression, where there was a rapid fall in GDP, unemployment rose from 0% to 25% within three years.

2.2.14.6. Lower Wages

In a recession, firms will also try to reduce costs by keeping wages low. Some workers—especially temporary workers without contracts—may experience wage cuts. This was a key feature of the 2008-2012 recession, which was also aggravated by rising living costs (e.g., higher taxes and oil prices). In 2020, at least cost-push inflation was expected to be low, aided by falling oil and commodity prices.

Another cause of lower wages is underemployment. Some workers may keep their jobs but experience reduced working hours. Instead of full-time employment, they may become part-time workers (e.g., working 20 hours a week). This means that while the rise in unemployment may appear muted, many workers experience significant reductions in effective income.

The self-employed are particularly vulnerable during a recession. In an economic downturn, they may quickly face cash-flow shortages and struggle to make ends meet.

2.2.14.7. Higher Government Borrowing

According to available information on www.economicshelp.org (2020), governments experience a fall in tax revenue during a recession due to:

- Firms making less profit, resulting in lower corporate tax revenue.
- Workers earning lower incomes, leading to lower income tax revenue.
- Declining house prices and fewer housing transactions, reducing stamp duty revenue.
- Lower consumer spending, leading to reduced VAT payments.

2.2.14.8. Government Spending

Governments see an increase in welfare spending during recessions due to rising unemployment benefits, housing benefits, and income support. Because of falling tax revenues and rising welfare payments (automatic fiscal stabilizers), a recession typically leads to an increase in the budget deficit and total government debt.

The U.S. budget deficit rose sharply following the 2008-09 recession. The forecast for 2021 was incorrect, as borrowing surged due to the impact of the COVID-19 pandemic and the impending recession.

Many countries saw a sharp rise in the budget deficit after the 2008 financial crisis because they had relied heavily on tax revenues from property and the finance sector. The collapse of the property market significantly impacted tax revenues. VAT receipts tend to be less cyclical.

A budget deficit may also increase if the government adopts expansionary fiscal policies to stimulate economic activity. For example, in 2010, the UK government reduced VAT.

2.2.14.9. Falling Asset Prices

Oil prices dropped sharply in 2008-09 and again in 2020. During a global recession, oil prices typically fall due to declining demand. The COVID-19 pandemic in 2020 caused a sharp drop in oil prices and a dramatic fall in share prices, reflecting analysts' expectations of severe economic downturns.

Falling asset prices contribute to the economic downturn. A decline in house prices creates a negative wealth effect, reducing consumer confidence and leading to further decreases in spending. A drop in house prices was anticipated in 2020.

2.2.14.10. Bond Yields

Usually, during a recession, government bond yields decline. This occurs because savings tend to rise, and investors prefer the security of bonds over the stock market. In 2020, U.S. bond yields fell to near-record levels, with the U.S. 2-year bond yield at 0.46%.

However, bond yields may rise if markets fear that the recession will lead to severe government liquidity shortages. For example, in 2020, Italian bond yields began to rise due to concerns about the collapse of the Italian economy. The response of the European Central Bank (ECB) and its willingness to inject liquidity would be crucial in determining the outcome.

2.2.14.11. Lost Output

A recession leads to lower investment, which can damage the economy's long-term productive capacity. If the recession is short-lived, the lost output may be limited, and the economy may recover quickly. However, during prolonged recessions, the damage is greater. The 2009 recession caused a permanent loss of output due to its severity and underlying structural weaknesses.

2.2.15. Impact of Recession on the Trend Rate of Economic Growth

2.2.15.1. Impact on Workers

In an article on the impact of recession on the trend rate of economic growth, the author argues that unemployment can have lasting negative effects.

First, unemployment is highly stressful and can damage a person's morale and health. Regions with high unemployment often experience increased social problems, including instability, riots, and vandalism. Mass unemployment can threaten a country's social fabric.

Unemployed individuals lose opportunities for skill development and on-the-job training. Long-term unemployment can make it harder for workers to secure future employment, leading some to drop out of the labor market entirely.

The author also suggests that unemployment and recessions can contribute to an increase in social and health issues, such as depression and suicide.

2.2.15.2. Impact on Firms

Firms experience reduced demand and lower profits. Some businesses may begin to incur losses and eventually go bankrupt. While some failures may be due to inefficiencies, others result from cyclical downturns and an inability to secure sufficient funding to survive the recession.

Recessions impact some industries more than others. For instance, there is usually a sharp decline in demand for luxury goods, such as foreign holidays and high-end sports cars, making firms in these sectors more vulnerable.

Companies with large reserves may withstand the recession, even if they experience temporary losses. However, many firms are forced to adopt aggressive strategies such as price wars and cost-cutting measures:

- Price Wars – Companies may aggressively lower prices to maintain market share, further reducing overall profitability.
- Cost Cutting – Declining profits force firms to reduce costs, which may involve closing unprofitable divisions and laying off employees.

2.2.15.3. Inequality

During a recession, inequality and relative poverty tend to worsen. Unemployment is a major contributor to relative poverty, as unemployed individuals experience a decline in income.

2.2.15.4. Potential Positive Effects of a Recession

The collapse of Chinese manufacturing in early 2020 led to a sharp drop in air pollution, potentially reducing pollution-related deaths.

Interestingly, some recessions have been linked to increased life expectancy. During the Great Depression, mortality rates in the U.S. fell in areas of high unemployment, possibly due to reduced spending on alcohol and cigarettes, as well as fewer traffic accidents (NPR – Great Recession led to lower mortality rates).

2.3. Empirical Review

Since the focus of this research is on leading organizational change during a recession, particularly the COVID-19-induced recession from 2019 to the present, it is pertinent to provide background insight into the onset, spread, and economic impact of COVID-19 on national economies. With ample literature on the subject of COVID-19, I will proceed to study and present other literature that emphasizes the imperative of leadership in navigating crisis situations engendered by recessions while ensuring organizational change and stability. In a discussion paper published by the IZA Institute of Labor Economics, titled *"A Literature Review of the Economics of COVID-19"*, the contributors, Abel Brodeur et al. (2020), posited that the spread of COVID-19 was expected to result in a considerable slowdown of economic activities. According to an early forecast by the International Monetary Fund (2020a), the global economy was projected to contract by about 3 percent in 2020, a contraction of far greater magnitude than that of the 2008-2009 Global Financial Crisis. However, in its latest update (June 2020), the International Monetary Fund (2020b) revised the forecast to a 4.9 percent contraction in 2020. The report cited the following reasons for the updated forecast: (i) greater persistence in social distancing activities, (ii) lower activity during lockdowns, (iii) a steeper decline in productivity among firms that had reopened for business, and (iv) greater uncertainty. The economic implications were expected to be wide-ranging and uncertain, with different effects on labor markets, production supply chains, financial markets, and the global economy. The negative economic effects varied depending on the stringency of social distancing measures (e.g., lockdowns and related policies), their duration, and the degree of compliance. Additionally, the pandemic and government interventions led to mental health distress, increased economic inequality, and disproportionately affected some socio-demographic groups.

The contributors revealed that the goal of their research was to survey the emerging literature on the economic consequences of COVID-19 and government responses and to synthesize insights from the growing number of studies. Figure 1 illustrates the number of National Bureau of Economic Research (NBER) working papers related to the pandemic released between March 2020 and May 2020. By the end of May, 106 papers on COVID-19 had been published. Similarly, over 60 discussion papers on the pandemic were released by the IZA Institute of Labor Economics.

2.3.1. History of Pandemics and Economic Impact

Pandemics are not new and have occurred at different stages in human history (Ferguson et al., 2020). While many outbreaks and human catastrophes have taken place, there has been a notable rise in the frequency of pandemics since the year 2000, primarily due to the increased emergence of viral diseases among animals (Madhav et al., 2017). Given this rise, many researchers, including Garrett (2007), Keogh-Brown et al. (2008), and more recently Madhav et al. (2017) and Fan et al. (2018), have argued that a large-scale global pandemic was inevitable. Ferguson et al. (2020) from the Imperial College London COVID-19 Response Team claimed that COVID-19 was the most serious pandemic since the 1918 Spanish Influenza. Despite comparisons, Barro (2020) concluded that the non-pharmaceutical interventions implemented during the 1918 Spanish Influenza pandemic were not successful in reducing overall deaths. This was because the interventions were not maintained for a sufficiently long period. He estimated that the mean duration of school closings and prohibitions on public gatherings was only 36 days, whereas the mean duration of quarantine and isolation was 18 days (0.05 years). These numbers were quite small compared to the duration of the 1918 Spanish Influenza pandemic.

Abel Brodeur et al. (2020) opined that pandemics are expected to have a severe negative impact on economic activities, at least in the short run. According to Jonas (2013), the impact includes: (i) avoidance reactions due to social distancing measures (e.g., individuals forgoing consumption and purchases of certain goods and services), (ii) small direct costs (e.g., hospitalization and medical expenses), (iii) larger indirect costs (e.g., loss of labor and production), and (iv) offsetting and cascading effects (e.g., disruption of services and travel). Several studies attempted to anticipate the economic loss from a pandemic.

In their citation, they mentioned that Jonung and Roeger (2006) forecasted that a hypothetical global pandemic would lead to a 1.6 percent drop in GDP for the European Union (EU) due to both demand- and supply-side factors. Other studies analyzed the impact through historical comparisons. For example, *how would the casualty numbers during the 1918 Spanish Influenza pandemic compare today?* Barro et al. (2020) estimated that, holding everything else constant, the 2.1 percent death rate during the 1918-1920 Spanish Influenza pandemic would translate to roughly 150 million deaths worldwide (compared to the world's population of 7.5 billion in 2020) during the COVID-19 pandemic. The authors also found that, on average, the 2.1 percent death rate corresponded to a 6 percent decline in GDP and an 8 percent fall in private consumption.

2.3.2. Evolution of COVID-19

According to Zhu et al. (2020), the first pneumonia case was discovered on December 8, 2019, in a wet market in Wuhan, the capital city of Hubei Province, China. Subsequently, several clusters of patients with similar pneumonia symptoms were reported throughout late December 2019.

The researchers noted that, compared to previous pandemics, COVID-19 had a disproportionate impact on the elderly from a health perspective. However, the lockdown measures were more global in scope and scale than those of previous pandemics, disrupting international supply chains as well as aggregate demand and consumption patterns. This, in turn, led to heightened financial market turbulence and amplified the economic shock. Moreover, greater borrowing and higher debt levels among firms and households during this period made the short-term economic shocks more potent compared to previous pandemics (Boissay & Rungcharoenkitkul, 2020).

2.3.3. Potential Economic and Financial Impacts of COVID-19

Abel Brodeur et al. further argued that to understand the potential negative economic impact of COVID-19, it is essential to examine the economic transmission channels through which the shocks will adversely affect the economy. They cited Carlsson-Szlezak et al. (2020a) and Carlsson-Szlezak et al. (2020b), who identified three main transmission channels. The first is the direct impact, related to the reduced consumption of goods and services. The prolonged duration of the pandemic and social distancing measures might reduce consumer confidence by keeping consumers at home, making them wary of discretionary spending and pessimistic about long-term economic prospects. The second is the indirect impact, which works through financial market shocks and their effects on the real economy. Household wealth will likely fall, savings will increase, and consumption spending will decrease further. The third consists of supply-side disruptions; as COVID-19 halts production, it negatively impacts supply chains, labor demand, and employment, leading to prolonged periods of layoffs and rising unemployment. In particular, Baldwin (2020) discusses the expectation shock, in which economic agents adopt a "wait-and-see" attitude. The author argues that this is common in economic climates characterized by uncertainties, as confidence in markets and economic transactions diminishes. Ultimately, the intensity of the shock is determined by the underlying epidemiological properties of COVID-19, consumer and firm behavior in the face of adversity, and public policy responses.

Gourinchas (2020, p. 33) summarizes the effect on the economy by stating: "A modern economy is a complex web of interconnected parties: employees, firms, suppliers, consumers, and financial intermediaries. Everyone is someone else's employee, customer, lender, etc." Due to the high degree of interconnectedness and specialization of productive activities, a breakdown in supply chains and circular flows will have a cascading effect.

Baldwin (2020) describes the impact of COVID-19 on the flow of income in the economy. First, households do not get paid, leading to reduced consumption and savings. The decrease in savings reduces investment and ultimately diminishes the capital stock. Second, households reduce their demand for imports, which in turn lowers income for the rest of the world, causing the country's exports to decline. Third, demand and supply shocks disrupt domestic and international supply chains. Fourth, all these shocks and disruptions result in a fall in output, reducing the use of factors of production. In this case, labor is more affected than capital due to reduced working hours or layoffs, leading to lower earnings.

It is also important to understand the processes that drive economic recoveries from crises. Carlsson-Szlezak et al. (2020a) explain different types of recovery through the concept of "shock geometry." There are three broad scenarios of economic recoveries, listed in ascending order of severity. First, the most optimistic scenario is labeled 'V-shaped,' in which aggregate output is displaced but quickly recovers to its pre-crisis path. Second, the 'U-shaped' path occurs when output drops swiftly but does not return to its pre-crisis trajectory, leaving a significant gap between the old and new output levels. Third, in the most severe 'L-shaped' scenario, output drops and growth rates continue to decline. In a dynamic model, the reduction in capital stock occurs in the next period, as seen in standard dynamic general equilibrium models.

Notably, Carlsson-Szlezak et al. (2020b) state that after previous pandemics, such as the 1918 Spanish Influenza, the 1958 Asian Influenza, the 1968 Hong Kong Influenza, and the 2002 SARS outbreak, economies have typically experienced 'V-shaped' recoveries. However, the COVID-19 economic recovery is not expected to be straightforward. This is due to the significant effects on employment caused by social distancing measures and lockdowns. According to Gourinchas (2020), within a short period, as much as 50 percent of the working population might be unable to find work. Moreover, even in the absence of containment measures, a recession would still occur, fueled by the precautionary and/or panic behavior of households and firms facing the uncertainty of a pandemic and an inadequate public health response (Gourinchas, 2020).

In an article titled "Crisis Leadership During the Great Recession of 2008," published in the *International Journal of*

Leadership and Change, the authors Steven M. Walker et al. (2016) mention that crisis leadership refers to actions taken by a leader to bring immediate change in the behavior, beliefs, and outcomes of individuals (Keller, 2000). Furthermore, crisis leadership is often practiced in response to an organizational crisis, which Lincoln (2005) defines as a low-probability, high-impact event that causes significant disruption or threat to an organization. Crisis leaders, particularly in the modern era, face many difficult decisions, as numerous factors exacerbate challenging situations, including media pressure, organizational chaos, and inaccurate information. Additionally, a leader must continuously scan the environment for potential crises (Thach, 2012). Leaders' responses to organizational crises will vary, resulting in both effective and ineffective actions, as some tasks will be managed well while others may fail (Prewitt, Weil, & McClure, 2011). Given the critical role of leaders during an organizational crisis—particularly in major events such as natural disasters, terrorist attacks, or a global economic collapse—it is important to analyze leadership responses to such crises to further the understanding of crisis leadership. Therefore, a critical aspect of this study is understanding the definition of a crisis, the economic crisis known as the Great Recession, and the concept of crisis leadership.

The Merriam-Webster Dictionary defines a crisis as "an unstable or crucial time or state of affairs in which a decisive change is impending, especially one with the distinct possibility of a highly undesirable outcome."

A crisis represents both the fragility and resilience of societies and organizations (Stern, 2013). Boin and Hart (2003) described crises as both dynamic and chaotic, representing a disruption of the organization in several ways. Furthermore, it is important to remember that a crisis threatens an organization's existence and can cause catastrophic damage, such as death, injuries, or harm to an organization's reputation (Mitroff, 2005). A crisis is an event that causes extreme distress to an organization, including the nation. Though a crisis can be an ambiguous event that varies based on the organization, several key actions should be considered, such as the need for quick decision-making and the recognition that inaction could cause catastrophic results, threatening the organization's priorities and increasing uncertainty (Van Wart & Kapucu, 2011). It is critical to understand the nature of a crisis. According to Fink (2000), a crisis can and will occur at any time, but a positive outcome is possible if it is handled appropriately. Contrary to Fink (2000), Lagadec (1993) argued that a crisis is preventable if its key elements are understood and guidelines are established to help leaders address it. Similarly, Boin and Hart (2003) stated that past crises could assist in preparedness and urgency for the situation at hand. Finally, Parker, Stern, Paglia, and Brown (2009) noted that both optimism and pessimism play important roles in preventing a crisis.

While the Great Recession officially began in December 2008, many economists consider September 2008 the crisis point. Within a period of two weeks, from September 15 through September 29, the financial services firm Lehman Brothers filed for Chapter 11 bankruptcy protection, and subsequently, the Dow Jones Industrial Average dropped 774 points. At the time of its filing, Lehman Brothers was the fourth-largest U.S. investment bank, and its bankruptcy filing remains the largest in U.S. history. Six months before the Lehman Brothers filing, regulators chose to bail out Bear Stearns, another competing investment bank. This eventually led to a Federal Reserve-led acquisition of Bear Stearns by JPMorgan Chase, preventing a total loss for shareholders (Michel, 2013). One day after Lehman Brothers' bankruptcy filing, the Federal Reserve announced that it would lend the insurance company American International Group (AIG) $85 billion to avoid its collapse. On September 26, 2008, Washington Mutual (WaMu), once the nation's largest savings and loan and the sixth-largest bank ("The 10 Largest," 2009), filed the second-largest bankruptcy in U.S. history. Thus, the economic crisis known as the Great Recession was born. However, it did not end with financial firms or during that month alone. The U.S. auto industry, which had previously been thriving, was also impacted when General Motors (GM) filed for Chapter 11 bankruptcy on June 1, 2009. GM's bankruptcy was the fourth-largest in U.S. history ("The 10 Largest," 2009). Another member of the U.S. "Big Three" automakers, Chrysler, sold most of its assets to the Italian automaker Fiat (Goldman, 2009). When all was said and done, the stock market lost over half its value by the first quarter of 2009, while housing prices fell by an average of 30%. Unemployment rose from 5% to 10% within a year (Eagan, 2014). The Gross Domestic Product (GDP) remained negative for seven consecutive quarters. The national debt increased from 67% of GDP to over 103%. All of these events occurred while Presidents Bush and Obama spent nearly $1.5 billion shoring up the economy through the Troubled Asset Relief Program (TARP) and the stimulus plan.

Yukl (2013) contended that, during a crisis, leaders' roles change as subordinates expect more from them. Leaders need to be decisive, assertive, and in charge of the group response. Additionally, they must communicate effectively with their teams. Hence, a discussion on crisis leadership follows. A crisis situation tests leaders and forces them to respond effectively to protect others and minimize consequences (Boin & Renaud, 2013). Kielkowski (2013) highlighted the crucial role of leadership in a crisis. Although a team effort is needed to overcome a crisis, the leader must guide the team and the organization through it, which is a challenging task (Ivanescu, 2011). An organizational crisis places tremendous pressure on leaders, resulting in them becoming either heroes or scapegoats (Boin & Hart, 2003). Therefore, understanding crisis leadership, as well as the traits and skills a leader should exhibit, is essential.

Crisis leadership refers to the actions leaders take to bring about immediate change in the behavior, beliefs, and outcomes of individuals (Keller, 2000). Several authors have provided insights into the roles and responsibilities of an effective crisis leader. These responsibilities range from critical thinking, sense-making, training and crisis preparation, creating loyalty, identifying organizational weaknesses, and modeling behavior (Hart, Tindall, & Brown, 2009; Jaques, 2012; Lawton, 2013; Mullins, 2003). Kielkowski (2013) added that communication with the team is essential for an effective response, which includes communication between leaders and followers, peers, and internal and external stakeholders. In addition to the characteristics of a leader in a time of crisis, the public has several expectations of leaders (Boin & Hart, 2003), including preparedness, warning others about the crisis, providing direction, showing empathy, and implementing lessons learned. These characteristics can serve a leader well and contribute to a successful post-crisis recovery. However, it is dangerous to use a crisis as an opportunity to push unnecessary reforms, and such actions should be avoided at all costs (Boin & Hart, 2003). It is also important to recognize the public's differing perceptions of public and private organizations during a crisis. The expectation is that private-sector leaders focus on competitive issues, while public-sector leaders should prioritize support and volunteer efforts to mitigate the crisis (Thach, 2012). Furthermore, during a crisis, it is crucial for leaders to acknowledge the existence of the crisis itself—that the worst-case scenario has materialized—and to take immediate action (Hart et al., 2009). Prewitt et al. (2011) recommended that leaders employ various techniques to manage the stress of crisis leadership. Discussing different types of leaders, Ivancevich, Konopaske, and Matteson (2005) noted that crisis-based leaders handle situations where prior knowledge and resources may be inadequate. Several researchers (Boin & Hart, 2003; Hart et al., 2009; Jaques, 2012; Lawton, 2013) have indicated that crises challenge leaders to develop new skills. By cultivating these attributes, crisis leadership can positively impact economic, existential, emotional, and spiritual outcomes, allowing leaders to learn and grow from crises (Mitroff, 2005).

One final distinction must be made—crisis leadership versus crisis management. While the terms are often used interchangeably in colloquial English, Wooten and James (2008) used the term "leadership competencies" to describe the knowledge, skills, and abilities needed for task performance. These include (a) decision-making, (b) communication, (c) creating organizational capabilities, (d) sustaining organizational culture, (e) managing multiple constituencies, and (f) developing human capital. Wooten and James further commented that these competencies help manage human resources as well as operational and strategic functions. Citing numerous authors, Wooten and James identified five phases of a typical business crisis: (a) signal detection, (b) preparation and prevention, (c) damage containment, (d) recovery, and (e) learning. Using a phenomenological approach, an understanding of Wooten and James' framework, in combination with Keller's (2000) definition, can assist in analyzing leaders' responses to the economic crisis known as the Great Recession of 2008 to gain further insights into the concept of crisis leadership.

In research conducted by Cecil Williams (2011), titled "Church Leaders' Financial Coping Strategies During a Recession," the researcher cited various authorities. According to her, economists have historically observed business cycles to make predictions about economic conditions. The author cited Stevenson and Wolfers (2011), who described a business cycle as a periodic movement in economic activity, measured by changes in economic factors such as GDP, unemployment rates, interest rates, inflation, and productivity. She posited that economists identified four stages of the business cycle: expansion, contraction, peaks, and troughs (Stevenson & Wolfers, 2011). The authors noted that business cycles do not follow a pattern and that neither their extent nor their duration is predictable.

According to Cecil Williams, economists have defined a recession as a phenomenon associated with the contraction stage of a business cycle (Stevenson & Wolfers, 2011). The literature suggests that there has been substantial debate regarding the nature of recessions. Economists have widely diverse opinions about the definition of a recession (Gaski, 2012). To determine when a recession begins and ends, it is necessary to agree on a definition (Gaski, 2012). Contemporary definitions of a recession have included the generalization that one indicator of a recession is a decline in a country's GDP for two consecutive quarters (Pump, 2012). Some business economists have historically linked stock market performance with the recognition of prerecession conditions in the economy (Lundquist & Stekler, 2012). Others have debunked the theory that sudden, steep drops in the stock market herald a recession (Lundquist & Stekler, 2012). Lundquist and Stekler (2012) urged caution when predicting a recession based on stock market drops. In some cases where a sharp decline in the stock market accompanies a recession, the decline began after the start of the recession.

A significant stock market decline could be a symptom of a recession, but it is not a reliable predictive factor (Lundquist & Stekler, 2012). Wang and Yang (2012) reported that some economists espoused an inverted yield curve as a predictive factor for recession. An inverted yield curve occurs when long-term investment yields fall below short-term deposit yields. The results of a study using an IS-LM model with the term structure of interest rates indicated that an inverted yield curve is not a reliable harbinger of a recession (Wang & Yang, 2012). Another major flaw in the theory was that long-term low interest rates could produce a nearly inverted yield curve (Wang & Yang, 2012). Based on the literature, it is difficult to define a recession, let alone predict when one will happen. Jorda, Schularick, and Taylor (2011) concluded that credit growth combined with depressed interest rates created conditions conducive to an economic recession.

The researcher cited an authority who stated that the 2009 recession surprised many government officials and, to a lesser extent, private sector financial experts (Mullard, 2011). The unprecedented worldwide economic prosperity in the previous two decades had created an expectation of continued success (Bhagwati, 2009). In 2008, the government offered an optimistic assessment of the U.S. economy (Mullard, 2011). Official press releases from the Office of the White House predicted continued low unemployment and economic strength despite slowing domestic growth. The government had high expectations that the $168 billion stimulus package, combined with lower interest rates, would reinvigorate the economy (Mullard, 2011). The government predicted that the stimulus package would provide continued economic growth at a slower pace (Mullard, 2011). A belief that the drop in housing and mortgage markets was contained and would hit bottom by mid-2008 supported the government's approach (Mullard, 2011). In early 2008, the majority of economists did not believe a recession was likely (Mullard, 2011). The prevailing opinion was that the science of economics had progressed to the point that a serious economic downturn could be averted (Mullard, 2011). Most economists, with a few dissenters, held that the stimulus plan was working and that the economy was rebounding (Mullard, 2011). The rapid economic decline in the latter part of 2008 quickly changed opinions about the stability of the economy (Mullard, 2011). Looking back on the events of 2008, economists concur that the stimulus plan likely prevented a worse financial disaster (Mullard, 2011). While many analysts were predicting that the United States would avoid a recession in 2008, the economy had already entered a recession (Imbs, 2010). In December 2008, the National Bureau of Economic Research (NBER), which determines the beginning and ending dates of recessions, announced that the United States was already in a recession, which had begun in December 2007 (Mullard, 2011).

The number of variables requiring assessment created a delay between the start of the recession and the determination that there was a recession. The assessment of some variables occurred after measuring their effects. In 2008, the labor market steadily declined, and the NBER cited this decline as a key factor in selecting the start date of the recession. By October 2008, there was a decline of 1.2 million U.S. jobs. Economists predicted an additional decline of 325,000 jobs for November (Mullard, 2011). Other factors used by the NBER included real personal income, industrial production, wholesale sales, retail sales, and GDP. The NBER analyzed the interaction of all these factors to determine the recession start date (Mullard, 2011). The NBER did not speculate on what caused the recession. The consensus among economic analysts pointed to the housing market downturn, which began in 2006, as the main cause of the recession (Mullard, 2011). There was a domino effect as housing prices tumbled, affecting home building and the sales of existing homes. Home foreclosure rates increased sharply, causing massive financial losses for banks, which in turn tightened access to credit for consumers (Mullard, 2011). The 2009 recession had the longest duration of any in the last 80 years. The NBER identified 10 official recessions between 1930 and 2008. Of those, only two recessions lasted for a year (Mullard, 2011).

President-Elect Barack Obama supported another stimulus package to boost the economy. Some economists predicted that the recession would extend into the second quarter of 2009 before the start of a recovery (Mullard, 2011). Other economists disagreed, predicting that a turnaround was imminent due to the stimulus spending already implemented by the government (Mullard, 2011). A $160 billion tax rebate in the first quarter of 2008 increased GDP in the following quarter (Daguerre, 2011). The financial market continued to decline, prompting the federal government to authorize trillions of dollars in emergency spending intended to stabilize the economy (Mullard, 2011). The measures included bailouts of banks and Wall Street firms totaling $700 billion. The Federal Reserve lent hundreds of billions of dollars to corporations and lenders as part of the package (Mullard, 2011). Some economists stated that stimulus spending was futile and that the recession would run its course regardless of attempts by the government to forestall the decline (Mullard, 2011). Within the literature, disagreement exists among economists regarding the probable length or severity of the recession. Denrell and Fang (2010) conducted a study to find out if economists could accurately predict economic conditions. The researchers examined past economic forecasts covering macroeconomic factors by 50 economists from 2002 to 2005 (Denrell & Fang,

2010). Their study aimed to determine which economists most accurately predicted significant outcomes. A comparison of overall accuracy versus significant event prediction showed that economists who were more accurate in predicting significant events had a lower overall accuracy rate (Denrell & Fang, 2010). Denrell and Fang suggested that less talented forecasters were more likely to make daring forecasts. An outrageous forecast that proved correct could establish the prognosticators' reputations and attract attention to their future predictions (Denrell & Fang, 2010). Denrell and Fang concluded that the results confirmed previous research casting doubt on the accuracy of forecasting (Denrell & Fang, 2010).

According to Kluth (2010), the economic recession had a negative effect on an increasing number of churches. The 2008 downturn affected industry leaders as the Lehman Brothers' bankruptcy undermined the country's financial structure (Rapp, 2009). The slowing of financial flow precipitated failure for several major companies and tremendous financial losses for others (Rapp, 2009). Construction and manufacturing accounted for nearly half of the total job losses during 2008 and 2009 (Hyatt & Erika, 2012). The reason these industries experienced disproportionate unemployment was that they relied heavily on financing to move products (Hyatt & Erika, 2012). The financial crisis in the United States had global repercussions, as the downturn deepened into a worldwide recession in 2009 (Rapp, 2009). Williams (2011) reported that many small business owners found it difficult to recover from the recession due to cash flow issues. Many suppliers sought quicker payments or higher deposits (Williams, 2011). Companies had less cash on hand to purchase inventories when the recession eased (Williams, 2011). Business leaders who managed to maintain cash reserves had a competitive advantage after the recession (Williams, 2011). The recession had a tremendous effect on church budgets from two fronts (Neroulias, 2011). Decreased income severely affected the finances of some churches. The recession also increased requests for assistance from parishioners and others (Marx & Davis, 2012).

In a 2010 national survey conducted by Faith Communities Today, 57% of respondents reported a significant decline in income due to the recession (Neroulias, 2011). The Hartford Institute for Religion Research, the Evangelical Council for Financial Accountability, and Christianity Today International all reported that larger churches were recovering from the recession more easily than smaller community churches. Larger churches recovered more quickly, in part, because of investment income, endowments, and the support of a larger membership (Neroulias, 2011). Incomes for smaller churches dropped disproportionately as the recession progressed, according to the reports. A 2010 survey of more than 11,000 congregations revealed that the recession had affected churches of all sizes. The survey results indicated that more than half a million church employees lost their jobs or had their salaries reduced because of the recession. Respondents also reported increased costs due to increased requests for assistance (Neroulias, 2011). Contributions to churches have decreased significantly in recent years (Ronsvalle & Ronsvalle, 2011). Based on a 2009 survey of 42 church denominations, donors have steadily reduced their church contributions as a percentage of gross income since 1968 (Ronsvalle & Ronsvalle, 2011). One major contributing factor to this trend was a shift in focus by church leaders from charitable causes to institutional maintenance (Ronsvalle & Ronsvalle, 2011). Church members were not as motivated to give more to support institutional maintenance as they were to support good works (Ronsvalle & Ronsvalle, 2011). Another factor cited was that many church members continued to contribute the same dollar amount to the church, even though their income had increased over time (Ronsvalle & Ronsvalle, 2011). One possible factor cited was that more people were utilizing other avenues for their charitable contributions (Ronsvalle & Ronsvalle, 2011).

Church leaders reduced allocations for charitable endeavors to an average of 35% of church income. Allocations for staff salaries and building maintenance, as a percentage of income, have remained steady for the past 20 years (Ronsvalle & Ronsvalle, 2011). Church spending on operations from 1968 to 2009 was reduced by 15%, and spending on charitable works was reduced by 47% (Ronsvalle & Ronsvalle, 2011). There were several reasons why the reduction in the percentage of spending for charitable works exceeded the reduction in spending for church operations (Ronsvalle & Ronsvalle, 2011). Costs for church operations increased due to inflation (Ronsvalle & Ronsvalle, 2011). The rising cost of healthcare and utilities had a significant impact on operational costs (Ronsvalle & Ronsvalle, 2011). As church income decreased, the rising operational costs reduced the amount of money available for charitable works (Ronsvalle & Ronsvalle, 2011). Contributions to charitable organizations with specific goals, such as the Salvation Army, have increased in recent years (Ronsvalle & Ronsvalle, 2011). People seemed more willing to contribute when there was a specific charitable goal (Ronsvalle & Ronsvalle, 2011). Some people allocated more of their charitable giving to nonchurch organizations and reduced their church donations (Ronsvalle & Ronsvalle, 2011). Donations to churches decreased sharply during the 2009 recession (Ronsvalle & Ronsvalle, 2011).

A previous study did not establish a link between economic downturns and contributions to churches (Ronsvalle & Ronsvalle, 2011). A consumer mindset has evolved among U.S. church members, fostering an expectation that the church exists to serve them rather than to transform them into individuals who serve others (Ronsvalle & Ronsvalle, 2011). Consumerism received some of the blame for the decrease in church donations by members as a percentage of income (Ronsvalle & Ronsvalle, 2011). As income increased from 1968 to 2009, people spent a higher percentage of their income on luxury items and consumer goods while contributing a lower percentage to the church (Ronsvalle & Ronsvalle, 2011). People over 25 tended to allocate a larger percentage of their charitable donations to nonchurch charities and educational institutions rather than to the church (Ronsvalle & Ronsvalle, 2011). One reason more people contributed to charities other than the church was the availability of choices (Ronsvalle & Ronsvalle, 2011). The church was once the only conduit for a person who wanted to support charitable works. Over time, people created organizations for a variety of causes (Ronsvalle & Ronsvalle, 2011). A person interested in a specific charitable cause could contribute to an organization that directly channeled support (Ronsvalle & Ronsvalle, 2011).

2.3.3.1. Change Strategies

Organizational change is one method of dealing with changes in the environment within which the organization operates (Boga & Ensari, 2009; Jimmieson & White, 2011; Shin et al., 2012). Both secular and religious organizations are affected by changes in the economy (Davis, Kee, & Newcomer, 2010; Kluth, 2010). When changes in the operating environment are rapid and extreme, organizations must react quickly to avoid surpassing the point of financial recovery (Austin, 2009).

Strategy is important in any economic climate, and strategic planning becomes even more critical when the economy is sluggish (Nafday, 2011). Some church leaders are reluctant to use the strategies employed by secular business leaders (Dobrai, 2010; Pearse, 2011; Santmire, 2010). Both secular and religious leaders face challenges to organizational survival due to economic concerns (Vaidyanathan & Snell, 2011). Some factors affecting both secular and religious organizations include new technologies, new knowledge, leadership changes, or the launch of new services (Beck, Lengnick-Hall, & Lengnick-Hall, 2008). The changing operating environment and globalization have increased challenges to business survival (Sheppard, 2012). Both business and nonprofit organizations face failure unless they acquire the necessary skills to manage operations efficiently and effectively (Yip, Twohill, Ernst, & Munusamy, 2010). Organizational resources, people, and processes must remain adaptable to cope with rapid change (Jimmieson & White, 2011; Patalano, 2011). The most effective leaders are adept at predicting change and making strategic adjustments in the organization, including the speed, direction, and intensity of the changes (Davis et al., 2010).

2.3.3.2. Resistance to Change

Some church leaders were unwilling to place emphasis on business issues, preferring to concentrate on the spiritual aspects of the institution (Pearse, 2011). This issue has significantly influenced the operational success of churches, as defined from a financial perspective (Pearse, 2011). Some church leaders separated secular business concerns, ignoring those that appeared to be at odds with religious principles (Pearse, 2011). Others in the religious community saw no conflict between secular business concerns and spirituality (Hardy & Ballis, 2005). A thorough examination of biblical passages on money revealed no dichotomy between spiritual pursuits and financial concerns in the church (Hardy & Ballis, 2005). Biblical teachings indicate that maintaining financial security is a necessary function of church leaders (Hardy & Ballis, 2005). Benning (2009) found that the separation of secular issues from spiritual aspects of the church was inadvertent rather than an intentional segregation. Pearse (2011) suggested that to facilitate growth, churches would need to adopt accepted secular business practices.

Congregations that emphasize increasing membership usually concentrate on generational preferences. This focus on generational preferences often results in prioritizing congregational expectations over spiritual concerns. The resulting shift in priorities provides a case for those opposing the intermingling of church operations with secular business practices (Pearse, 2011). Internal strife about applying secular business practices can create challenges for church leaders seeking change (Pearse, 2011). Internal change within the religious community is sometimes difficult to implement due to member resistance (Pearse, 2011). Wrenn (2011) examined resistance to change within religious organizations, particularly regarding marketing strategies. Challenges to existing paradigms often resulted in resistance to change (Van Dijk & Van Dick, 2009; Weiner, Belden, Bergmire, & Johnston, 2011; Wrenn, 2011). Van Dijk & Van Dick (2009) opined that arbiters of change within an organization must be aware of resistance to change. Specific patterns of resistance were likely to occur regardless of the nature of the change. These patterns emerged due to specific causes, and identifying them made it possible to initiate countermeasures to lessen resistance to change (Van Dijk & Van Dick, 2009).

One common complaint was that the change was merely the latest in a series of initiatives launched as the next great plan, only to be discarded soon after. The countermeasures for this included minimal fanfare, leadership support, assigned change leaders, and the integration of change into daily operations (Van Dijk & Van Dick, 2009). Van Dijk and Van Dick's (2009) study identified several other complaints that led to resistance to change and the corresponding countermeasures. The study indicated that resistance to change is usually an emotional rather than an intellectual response (Van Dijk & Van Dick, 2009). It is important to recognize that emotional issues cannot be overcome using facts and data (Foster, 2010; Van Dijk & Van Dick, 2009; Weiner et al., 2011). Gaining people's support for change is cost-effective when they feel emotionally secure that it is the right decision (Van Dijk & Van Dick, 2009).

Balancing church members' expectations against financial realities will likely require fundamental changes in churches' fiscal policies (Notarantonio & Quigley, 2009). There is no standard practice among church leaders regarding financial policy. Some church leaders regard secular business practices as incompatible with the spiritual message they wish to convey (Wrenn, 2011). Hardy and Ballis (2005) noted that most church leaders seek to separate secular and spiritual issues. Dobrai (2010) observed that in cases where secular and spiritual concerns are formally separated, church leaders often reject secular business practices that could be beneficial.

Church leaders developed better relationships with parishioners when interactions increased (Son & Wilson, 2011). One way to increase interactions with parishioners is to persuade them to volunteer and get involved in church operations (Son & Wilson, 2011). Parishioners of all ages are more likely to volunteer when they agree with the church's mission (Dobrai, 2010). Parishioners involved in church operations are also more likely to contribute financially (Dobrai, 2010). Effectively communicating the church's mission increased volunteerism among parishioners (Son & Wilson, 2011). Stakeholders identified with an organization as they gained more understanding of its mission and goals (Balmer, 2008). Identifying with the organization, in turn, influences how stakeholders act toward the organization (Balmer, 2008).

2.3.3.3. Recession Strategies

Jagusztyn (2009) stated that a recession creates opportunities for innovation. Companies' leadership tends to operate on autopilot in good economic times. Recessions force company leaders to look for new ways to gain a competitive advantage. Company leaders who focus on competitors rather than customers do not fare as well (Jagusztyn, 2009). The way to gain a competitive advantage in a recession is to innovate and be a market leader rather than a follower. Success during a recession depends on outlook. Instead of waiting for a recovery, company leaders who succeeded made their own recovery. They looked for the opportunities created by the recession (Jagusztyn, 2009). There were some key areas important to success in a recession. Customer service is more important than ever. Company leaders who neglect to build customer service will find they have few customers when the recession ends (Jagusztyn, 2009).

Another area identified as important was technology. The internet has created an interconnected global community. Company leaders who fail to take advantage of the internet and other technologies will lose a competitive edge in a recession (Ifinedo, 2011; Jagusztyn, 2009). Another key for survival during a recession is to be aware of changes in the financial environment and make appropriate strategy changes. The way to succeed in a recession is to reinvent the business because a return to pre-recession conditions is not likely to occur (Jagusztyn, 2009). Davis et al. (2010)

advocated strategic change on a continuing basis to assure the survival of the church. The traditional expectations of what the church should be have changed (Davis et al., 2010). Increased access to communications and improved education has resulted in many church members questioning the traditional church management hierarchy (Davis et al., 2010). There was a growing movement to embrace current trends as well as include church members in the decision-making process (Davis et al., 2010). The internet has increased the church's customer base as well as increased competition for customers. Davis et al. (2010) observed that the pace of change is increasing and that constant adjustment to strategies is necessary for the survival of the church. The recession was the latest challenge to face the church. Church leaders needed to make strategy changes as the recession changed the economic environment (Davis et al., 2010).

Allio (2010) discussed the threats and opportunities of the recession for CEOs. The recommended course of action included a review of new threats. Allio (2010) also recommended conducting an analysis of how other leaders in the industry coped with these threats. One opportunity identified was to initiate a formal process for continuous innovation throughout the value chain (Allio, 2010). Another opportunity was to identify ways to manage transparency in the organization. Customer management was a significant imperative (Allio, 2010). Another opportunity was to accept that other companies may do certain things better and to use the superior method. Allio (2010) suggested the use of external collaboration. Allio (2010) recommended some opportunities for managers. Allio (2010) recommended the use of Twitter to communicate with frontline supervisors to keep them informed. Another recommendation was the proactive use of the internet to build brand loyalty, a tactic already employed by Nike's management team (Allio, 2010).

Waters (2007) recommended the use of the internet for communications and fundraising by church leaders. Allio (2010) recommended that CEOs consider a variety of innovations to reduce costs and improve productivity. Investments in technology have proven to reduce labor costs (Allio, 2010). Outsourcing of design, production, or distribution functions has worked for many firms to increase competitive advantage. New technologies, such as cloud computing for IT operations, present potential opportunities to manage costs (Allio, 2010). Allio (2010) discussed the implementation of new process methodologies to increase customer satisfaction. Allio (2010) discussed design-driven innovation, which is a process in which designers try to develop products that will appeal to customers emotionally. Procter & Gamble successfully used design-driven innovation to increase competitive advantage.

A similar process involves gaining a competitive advantage by offering personalized customer experiences. Allio (2010) stated that when there is internal resistance to innovation, it might be necessary for CEOs to seek strategic alliances to facilitate innovation creation. Successful collaborations have occurred throughout the value chain. Toyota management used value chain collaboration to create success for the company. Netflix offered a $1 million incentive to anyone who could develop a method to increase the company's customer movie recommendation feature by 10% or more. After an analyst group claimed the prize, Netflix officials stated that they plan to repeat the offer (Allio, 2010). Ling (2010) conducted a study through interviews with contractor firm managers to identify recession strategies. Company leaders have taken extraordinary measures to cope with the effects of the recession. The study results identified three distinct types of strategy: contracting-related, cost control, and financial (Ling, 2010). The results of the study showed that most contractors placed bids for more projects within their capability and resources. All of the participants responded that tighter controls were implemented for waste, financial management, and purchasing (Ling, 2010). Most of the managers reported that they had frozen salaries, suspended hiring, and established a reserve fund to cover unforeseen expenses (Ling, 2010). Previous studies of contractors' actions during recessions revealed common actions that included diversification into other markets, tighter financial management, relationship building with clients, lower prices, marketing enhancement, strategy planning, minimizing staff overlap, and concentration on core efficiencies (Ling, 2010).

Navarro (2009) stated that, with readily available information, managers could predict business cycles accurately enough to create forecasting models. Managers who used accurate forecasting models could have a competitive advantage over their competitors (Navarro, 2009). Some of the variables included in the available information were stock prices, the Economic Cycle Research Institute weekly report, and the bond market yield curve (Navarro, 2009). The addition of business cycle forecasting allowed managers to make better tactical decisions, such as inventory, pricing, and marketing. Business cycle forecasts also helped managers make better strategic decisions regarding topics such as expansions and capital investments (Navarro, 2009). Navarro (2009) noted that many items found in daily financial newspapers were helpful when forecasting business cycles. Executive teams can learn to interpret forecasting data and create business cycle forecasts (Navarro, 2009). Company managers who learn to predict business cycles gain a competitive advantage and can minimize the effects of a recession on their organization (Navarro, 2009).

After the 2001 recession, there was a common belief that future recessions were unlikely due to refined government monetary policies that reined in business cycles. The Federal Reserve System's policies that contributed to the 2008 recession showed that government policies could not tame business cycles (Navarro, 2009). Since the onset of the 2009 recession, there has been renewed interest in implementing business cycle forecasts into business strategy planning (Navarro, 2009). Business professionals and academics have focused considerable research on the identification of the factors that influence business cycles (Navarro, 2009). In several areas, managers could employ business cycle forecasting for competitive advantage (Navarro, 2009). Managers could use business cycle forecasting to predict movement and key turning points in the business cycle. Predicting key turning points in the business cycle could allow managers to apply strategies and tactics to make the best use of company resources (Navarro, 2009). The management team may either develop their own business cycle forecasting system or use an outside consulting firm. The use of an outside consulting firm could also complement the in-house system. Navarro (2009) developed a business cycle forecasting method that uses readily available information to create forecasts. The information included daily and weekly financial publications. One important source included in the data is a GDP forecasting equation. Other data sources in the business cycle forecasting method include stock market trends and the bond market yield curve. Several studies have validated the accuracy of Navarro's (2009) business cycle forecasting method.

2.3.4. Recession Strategies for Competitive Advantage

Reeves and Deimler (2009) offered strategies to help companies survive and gain a competitive advantage during a

recession. The uncertainty and unpredictability that persist after a recession ends will continue to influence the business environment (Reeves & Deimler, 2009). Company leaders who can anticipate and react to significant shifts in the business landscape will have a distinct competitive advantage. Reeves and Deimler (2009) recommended integrating lessons learned during a recession into the company's strategic plan. The consensus among business professionals, economists, and government leaders was that the post-recession business environment would remain significantly different from what it was before the recession.
Reeves and Deimler (2009) predicted that traditional business strategies would not be effective for gaining a competitive advantage after the recession ended. Many firms employed conventional recession tactics during the 2008 recession, such as reducing production, downsizing labor, cutting spending, and conserving cash reserves (Reeves & Deimler, 2009). Waiting out the recession has been a proven strategy when the economy returns to its prior state and competitors follow the same approach. However, there was a growing consensus that the recession would persist and that the business environment was unlikely to revert to its previous state (Reeves & Deimler, 2009).

Economists predicted that the recession would accelerate the demise of ineffective business models, lead to industry-wide restructuring, alter investor strategies, and change consumer behavior. Additionally, far-reaching government regulations that significantly impact the business environment were anticipated (Reeves & Deimler, 2009). In such a business climate, a passive waiting strategy placed companies at risk of being overtaken by aggressive competitors. Reeves and Deimler (2009) did not recommend a defensive strategy for the long-term survival of a company. Instead, they proposed a two-part approach: first, implementing specific short-term and medium-term strategies to promote business growth during the recession, and second, integrating the lessons learned into the company's strategic plan after the recession ended (Reeves & Deimler, 2009).

The primary objective was the company's survival. The survival plan included cost reductions, efficiency improvements, financial management, organizational restructuring, and process enhancements. External factors such as customer retention and credit management were also considered. Strategic management involved capital investment decisions and the divestiture of non-core assets (Reeves & Deimler, 2009). While survival strategies alone do not secure a competitive advantage, companies that experienced growth during a recession historically maintained their competitive edge once the recession ended. After implementing defensive measures, management should develop strategies to ensure a competitive advantage post-recession (Reeves & Deimler, 2009). One recommended strategy was offering new services (Reeves & Deimler, 2009). For example, during the 1989 recession, U-Haul faced increased price competition. Unable to counter competitors' low-price strategies, the company began selling cardboard boxes and packing materials to customers. These high-margin offerings helped U-Haul achieve a 10% operating margin, compared to the industry standard of 3% (Reeves & Deimler, 2009).

Alternative pricing models were another recommendation. Before 1980, airlines purchased aircraft engines outright, with replacement parts and labor as additional costs. GE and Rolls-Royce introduced a new model, providing airlines with engines at no initial cost while charging a by-the-hour fee for maintenance. This strategy allowed both companies to increase their market share and profit margins (Reeves & Deimler, 2009).

Another recommendation was entering new markets and exiting others. The 1991 recession led to a decline in the luxury car market. In response, Porsche introduced the Boxster at 60% of the price of their 911 model. This strategic move increased Porsche's revenue by 46% (Reeves & Deimler, 2009). Reeves and Deimler (2009) also advised companies to seek opportunities to acquire recession-weakened rivals and to consider forming strategic alliances with suppliers, customers, or competitors.

2.3.5. Strategic Planning in the Church during a Recession

The success of strategic planning in the church depends on aligning goals with the congregation's existing culture (Manala, 2010). Some church leaders view the church as a business operation and do not find integrating secular business practices problematic (Dobrai, 2010; Pearse, 2011). Others, however, see the use of secular business strategies as inappropriate for a religious institution (Beck, Lengnick-Hall, & Lengnick-Hall, 2008). The opinions of church members play a key role in determining the extent to which church leaders integrate secular business models into church operations (Dobrai, 2010).

Some advocates support incorporating proven secular business practices into church operations, provided they do not conflict with church principles (Dobrai, 2010; Hardy & Ballis, 2005). Conversely, some church leaders oppose such integration, believing it directly contradicts biblical teachings (Watson & Scalen, 2008). Debate continues regarding the benefits of integrating secular business practices, as they are not always immediately apparent (Watson & Scalen, 2008). Discussions also persist about which business practices are appropriate and where they should be applied within church operations (Dobrai, 2010; Watson & Scalen, 2008).

Some church leaders believe business practices should not be implemented in church operations (Dobrai, 2010). Critics argue that a secular business model, which emphasizes profit, is too rigid and impersonal for church functions (Dobrai, 2010). Additionally, some church leaders are hesitant to discuss financial matters with parishioners, as they struggle to reconcile spiritual and fiscal responsibilities. This reluctance may unintentionally diminish the perceived importance of financial issues among church members (Dobrai, 2010). Parishioners may interpret the avoidance of financial discussions as a separation between spiritual and financial responsibilities, potentially leading to decreased financial support for the church (Benning, 2009). However, some church leaders view all aspects of church operations, including financial matters, as equally important (Dobrai, 2010).

Studies indicate that church leaders often fail to communicate their financial management positions to the congregation (Benning, 2009). A lack of transparency regarding how donations are allocated can result in diminished trust (Van Iwaarden, Van Der Wiele, Williams, & Moxham, 2009). Increased financial transparency, on the other hand, has been shown to boost donations (Dobrai, 2010). Trust is essential for fostering group cohesion and securing support for a shared vision and goals (Yi Feng Chen, Chen-Ho Chao, & Tjosvold, 2010). A well-defined mission statement serves as a valuable tool for establishing financial priorities (Khalifa, 2011).

Concerns persist that incorporating secular business practices may compromise the church's mission in favor of operational efficiency (Wrenn, 2011). However, business practices—such as budgeting and accounting infrastructure—

equip church leaders with essential tools to manage resources effectively and achieve their goals (Watson & Scalen, 2008).

2.3.6. Communication and Change Facilitation

Rankinen et al. (2009) identified communication as one of the keys to success in any organization. Church leaders must communicate the mission to the congregation, and congregation members must communicate their expectations to church leaders (Rankinen et al., 2009). A mission statement provides a means of communicating the church's mission and values to the congregation (Olison & Roloff, 2008). After the creation of a mission statement, it is advisable to expand it to include goals (Olison & Roloff, 2008). Congregation members who are knowledgeable about church operations are more likely to support church leaders' decisions (Dobrai, 2010). Some key information recommended for communication to the congregation includes goals, mission, financial performance, achievements, and failures (Olison & Roloff, 2008). Communication with the congregation should be ongoing in order to maintain trust and support (Olison & Roloff, 2008). Incorporating the secular business practice of aligning goals with processes into church operations helps create open lines of communication (Pearse, 2011). A concise mission statement can help prevent conflicts of priorities (Firmin & Gilson, 2010). Church leaders and parishioners can work together to set priorities and goals that support the church mission (Manala, 2010), and communication can help facilitate change (Rankinen et al., 2009). Some have argued that the rise of consumerism has reduced the mission of the church to a commodity (Santmire, 2010). Consumerism places a premium on the accumulation of money and possessions to the extent that other activities are neglected (Santmire, 2010). Consumerism may affect the way parishioners measure a church's success (Santmire, 2010).

The consumerist point of view makes communication with parishioners more important than ever, including articulating a robust mission statement (Khalifa, 2011). Strategic communications help church members understand the service, value, and impact of the organization. The church communication infrastructure should also include a feedback mechanism regarding mission performance (Morgan, 2008). Church leaders should examine congregants' expectations to determine if they align with the church mission and the religious tenets of the organization (Dobrai, 2010).

A case study by Schwartz (2011) identified 13 steps to improve volunteerism. Schwartz (2011) based the study on results experienced by New York Cares, an organization that runs volunteer programs for more than 1,000 nonprofit groups, coordinating more than 50,000 volunteers. Communication is one of the keys to the success of New York Cares (Schwartz, 2011). According to Schwartz (2011), the same strategies, based on 13 key points that made New York Cares successful, would work for other nonprofits seeking volunteers. Targeted communication on a regular basis is important for developing a strong volunteer base (Schwartz, 2011).

A business strategy must be successfully implemented in order to be effective (Bryson, Crosby, & Bryson, 2009). Strategy planning and strategy implementation are integrated concepts, and an effective strategy planning session must include an outline for the implementation of the plan (Bryson et al., 2009). A strategic plan can serve as a roadmap to move the organization from its current condition to the desired state (Bryson et al., 2009). The plan must not be so rigid as to prevent necessary adjustments (Bryson et al., 2009). Leaders must plan execution simultaneously with the formulation of the strategic plan (Austin, 2009). The concept of strategic planning is not new (Mintzberg et al., 2008; Taylor et al.,

2008); however, it was not formalized as a scholastic discipline until the 1960s. Ten different models of strategic planning have been identified (Mintzberg et al., 2008). These ten models form three groups: rationalist, evolutionary, and process-based. Prior to the formalized design of strategic planning, managers relied on rational assumptions to formulate plans (Mintzberg et al., 2008). Strategic planning has evolved into a formal process with a number of theories and models that can serve as powerful tools for church survival (Pearse, 2011). Strategic management is cited as being equally important to faith-based nonprofit organizations and secular businesses (Kong, 2008). Kong (2008) concluded that some important considerations for nonprofit organization leaders include creating a strategic management plan that allows the organization to maintain independence and pursue social missions. Strategic planning is a complex process that, in order to be effective, requires leaders to develop a holistic view of the organization and consider all aspects as integral to the plan (Mintzberg et al., 2008). Additionally, the strategic plan must constantly evolve in response to both internal and external changes in the operating environment (Mintzberg et al., 2008). It is important to keep the strategic plan simple (Kong, 2008). An effective plan should establish a clear definition of the strategy, set measurable goals, and identify resources (Kong, 2008). Leaders must communicate the plan to all levels of the organization (Kong, 2008). They must also put a monitoring system in place to keep the plan on track (Kong, 2008). Historically, the majority of strategic plans failed within the first year after implementation (Austin, 2009). Various reasons cited for the high failure rate include factors such as the complexity of the plan or attempting to implement changes too quickly (Austin, 2009). The human element is another factor to consider in strategic plan implementation

(Pearse, 2011). Difficulties in implementation are often associated with resistance to change. A lack of effective communication regarding the change is also cited as a challenge (Pearse, 2011). Effectively communicating change to all stakeholders while simultaneously managing changes, monitoring progress, and obtaining feedback presents a significant challenge (Pearse, 2011). One of the problems organizational leaders often encounter when using traditional strategy implementation techniques is that they place emphasis on structure while disregarding important elements such as culture, people, control systems, and instruments (Weiner et al., 2011). One major factor that interferes with successful strategic planning implementation is that leaders focus on the planning phase but lack the skills to implement the strategy (Austin, 2009). Another frequently cited problem is that some managers focus on short-term gains rather than long-term advantages, resulting in a lack of commitment to the success of the strategic plan (Pearse, 2011). The outcomes of strategic planning often fail to meet expectations because the organizational structure fails to align with the strategic plan and its implementation (Bryson et al., 2009). When a strategic plan fails, it is often due to a failure to link the plan to an effective implementation (Bryson et al., 2009). The strategic plan should have clear, achievable goals (Bryson et al., 2009). Successful implementation of the strategic plan depends on communicating these goals to all levels of the organization (Bryson et al., 2009).

2.3.7. Organizational Strategy and Leadership

Heavey and Murphy (2012) posited that organizational leaders should review their current business strategies to determine whether they are adequate to handle economic disruptions. Effective strategic planning involves targeting specific gaps revealed during an analysis and assessment of the organization (Heavey & Murphy, 2012). Relying on intuition is not an effective strategic planning methodology. Assessing the organization requires utilizing a holistic approach. A piecemeal assessment often fails to detect important linkages that affect desired outcomes (Heavey & Murphy, 2012). Management strategies created for a more robust economy may become ineffective as the economic environment changes. Effective organizational leadership requires the development of established metrics to measure important factors (Heavey & Murphy, 2012).

Pearse (2011) discussed strategy analysis to determine the current state of the church and compared the results with church leaders' expectations. The analysis included an examination of both internal and external factors (Pearse, 2011). It is important to communicate church leaders' strategies for accomplishing both vision and mission (Pearse, 2011). Church leaders often see their role as that of a spiritual advisor; however, they must also assume the role of a business manager (Dobrai, 2010; Watson & Scalen, 2008). Systems management and strategic planning are as important to a church as they are to secular businesses (Dobrai, 2010; Watson & Scalen, 2008).

Raza and Standing (2011) discussed the importance of recognizing and managing resistance to organizational change. Successful change includes addressing stakeholders' concerns as a dynamic process. Aligning stakeholder concerns and conflict resolution efforts is essential to successful strategy implementation (Raza & Standing, 2011).

Implementing a strategic plan will help church leaders improve financial stability (Dobrai, 2010). A church leader who cannot maintain financial viability is unlikely to remain focused on the mission (Dobrai, 2010).

A survey of more than 125,000 people revealed that 60% of respondents believed their organization was poor at strategy execution (Neilson, Martin, & Powers, 2008). The reason was that organizations failed to translate important strategic or operational decisions into actions. Companies that failed at execution generally focused on the management structure or motivation but failed to address the root causes of problems (Neilson et al., 2008). Critical factors in strategy execution include identifying responsibility for implementation and granting the authority to make decisions. Once these two factors are in place, structure and motivation alignment follow (Neilson et al., 2008).

Strategic planning has been gaining prominence in church operations. Many church leaders are embracing strategic planning as a tool for effective management (Pearse, 2011). Church strategic planning also includes guidance on why the church exists. The authors recommended that church strategic plans include strategies to create positive effects on the local community within three to five years. The recommended strategic plan for church management would combine spiritual and business elements to map a course toward achieving desired goals (Pearse, 2011). The strategic plan would form the framework from which annual and multiyear plans would be developed (Pearse, 2011).

The church strategic plan should establish the course and priorities for the organization while being adaptable to internal changes and improvements in the operating environment. The plan should provide a pathway to accomplishing the mission set by church leaders within a specified time frame. It must also maintain the organization, care for church members, and grow membership.

Church planning includes three phases:
(a) Information gathering—collecting and analyzing data about past performance and the current internal and external environment.
(b) The actual planning phase—reviewing the mission, vision, goals, and values.
(c) Presentation of the strategic plan to church leaders for approval or modification.

Once the strategic plan is accepted, implementation involves monitoring specific performance measures. The final step is the presentation of the strategic plan to the congregation for approval (Pearse, 2011).

2.3.8. Types of Organizational Change

According to Ahmed AL Shebi (2016), in his research work *A Strategic Framework for Managing Transformational Change: Towards Sustainability in the Abu Dhabi Public Sector Organization*, there are many ways of looking at organizational change. He categorized organizational change into the following:

2.3.8.1. Planned Change

This type of organizational change is intentional, with corporate planning provided for expected changes. In this approach, organizational change is viewed as a process of transitioning from one state to another through a series of preplanned steps. Planning is based on the assumption that the organization operates in a stable and predictable environment. According to the researcher, the main emphasis is on a preplanned, rational, centralized, and systematic change process. However, he acknowledged that the primary criticism of this approach is the difficulty in predicting the stability of the organizational environment due to its dynamic nature (Teece, 2012).

2.3.8.2. Emergent Change

The author noted that the popularity of the emergent theory of change increased with criticism of the planned approach. The emergent approach is more recent and is considered more practical than the incremental approach. In this perspective, change is viewed as a continuous, unpredictable, and constant process that any organization may encounter.

Emergent change, according to the author, is implemented as a bottom-up approach where employees are facilitated by divisional managers. All employees are prepared to face change and are trained with the necessary skills and competencies to operate in a dynamic environment. The author cited Brown (2005), who stated that emergent change relies on effective communication, high cooperation, and collaboration between management and employees.

Incremental Change: Al Shebi (2016) explained that incremental change is an advanced version of planned change. According to him, the difference is that planning is done logically, while changes are implemented incrementally. This often involves changes in response to the external environment. Generally speaking, in this approach, managers attempt to align organizational performance and service offerings after analyzing environmental needs. A gap analysis is conducted, and appropriate corrective actions are taken. Compared to other models, this approach is not considered a "blinded" method. He further cited James Quinn (1978), who, in his theory of "Logical Incrementalism," presents a similar concept regarding strategy development in a changing environment. He noted that the main criticism of this model is its inability to cope with drastic organizational changes (Brown, 2005; Bock et al., 2012). He believes that the particular strength of this type of change lies in its continuous progression rather than a "frame-breaking burst" approach, which affects one organizational section instead of transforming the entire organization. According to the author, incremental changes maintain the existing equilibrium rather than achieving a new one, function through the normal structure rather than creating a new one, and involve technological improvements rather than breakthrough advancements (Lau, 2010).

Stepped Change: The researcher opines that this kind of change occurs when the trend line of a particular factor stops being smooth, resulting in a significant upward or downward shift. Step change, according to him, is not feasible for every organization, as the structure does not always allow for it unless specifically undertaken. He asserts that it is difficult to predict in advance, as strategic planning has shifted from trend analysis toward scenario planning (Randall, 2004).

Transformational Change: The researcher asserts that Johnson and Scholes (2010) argue that, given the complexities and the highly competitive nature of the external environment, every organization should be able to handle radical, drastic changes. They further state that radical change is involved when an organization operates in a manner that is currently outside its existing paradigm. The researcher notes that this clearly involves a drastic cultural shift to succeed, which is one of the main criticisms of this type of change. He cited Ashburner et al. (1996), who emphasized the need to gather a comprehensive view of targeted transformational change before opting for it. In the process, five key aspects are suggested as indicators for assessing the feasibility of transformational change (Brau, 2006). These include the existence of multiple and interrelated changes across the system as a whole, the creation of new organizational forms at a collective level, the creation of roles at the individual level, the reconfiguration of power relations (especially the formation of new leadership groups), and the creation of a new culture, ideology, and organizational meaning. He also cited Ferlie et al. (1996), who agreed and argued that transformational change surpasses strategic change in every way, as it aims to alter the organization at its core. They emphasized the importance of evaluating four key issues: perceptions regarding employee value, attitudes toward knowledge creation, attitudes toward refining the application process, and perceptions of motivation as crucial for achieving transformational change (Clegg et al., 2011).

Radical Change: According to the researcher, this type of change involves fundamentally altering an "accepted" or "taken-for-granted" situation on a large scale, such as changing the state of the economy or social structure. This type of change rarely occurs within an organization, as it may encounter strong resistance.

The researcher revealed that Authenticity Consulting (2005), from a practitioner's perspective, has reclassified and operationalized the various types of change into four specific categories:

- Organization-Wide Versus Subsystem Change: Examples of organization-wide change might include major restructuring, collaboration, or "rightsizing." Organizations must often undertake organization-wide change to evolve to a different stage in their life cycle, such as transitioning from a highly reactive, entrepreneurial organization to one with more stability and planned development. Experts assert that successful organizational change requires a shift in culture—cultural change is another example of organization-wide change. Examples of subsystem change might include the addition or removal of a product or service, the reorganization of a specific department, or the implementation of a new process to deliver products or services.

- Transformational Versus Incremental Change: An example of transformational (or radical, fundamental) change might be altering an organization's structure and culture from a traditional top-down, hierarchical model to one with a significant number of self-directing teams. Another example is Business Process Re-engineering, which attempts to deconstruct (at least theoretically) the major components and processes of the organization before reassembling them in a more optimal manner. Transformational change is sometimes referred to as quantum change. Examples of incremental change might include continuous improvement as part of a quality management process or implementing a new computer system to enhance efficiency.
- Remedial Versus Developmental Change: Change may be intended to remedy current situations, such as improving the poor performance of a product or the entire organization, reducing workplace burnout, making the organization more proactive and less reactive, or addressing large budget deficits. Remedial projects often seem more focused and urgent, as they address pressing problems. The success of these projects is often easier to determine since the problem is either resolved or not. Conversely, change can also be developmental—aimed at making an already successful situation even more successful, such as expanding the customer base or replicating successful products or services. Developmental projects can appear more general and ambiguous than remedial ones, depending on how specific their goals are and how important achieving them is to organizational members. Some individuals

may perceive that if developmental changes are not made soon, remedial changes will become necessary.

- Unplanned Versus Planned Change: Unplanned change usually occurs due to a major, sudden surprise to the organization, causing members to respond in a highly reactive and disorganized manner. Examples of unplanned change include the sudden departure of a Chief Executive Officer, significant public relations crises, poor product performance leading to rapid customer loss, or other disruptive events. Planned change, on the other hand, occurs when organizational leaders recognize the need for a major transformation and proactively devise a plan to achieve it. Planned change is implemented through strategic plans, reorganizations, or other structured initiatives. However, despite careful planning, planned change often unfolds in a more chaotic and disruptive manner than participants anticipate.

2.3.9. Resistance to Organizational Change

According to Al Shebi (2016), resistance is part and parcel of change management. He cited Dent and Goldberg (1999), who stated that it has become a well-established mental model. Gary Evans (2004) posits that organizational change has a broader scope compared to hiring a new employee. He equally avers that it involves adopting adaptive measures in various aspects of organizational life, such as organizational culture, work processes, and job responsibilities. Such change can lead to an overall transformation if radical programs are implemented. Reasons for change in the workplace may include the implementation of a strategy to achieve certain goals, transitioning to a different method of operations, adjusting to the effects of an external force, and the designation of a new leader or manager whose work ethic could affect the entire organization or unit (Evans, 2004).

Mark Ahn et al. (2004) opined that change in an organization affects not only its structure and culture but also the personal management styles of its leaders. As such, managing change is an essential part of leadership. One element that he and his colleagues mentioned in their study is the role of the 'business press' in featuring corporate leaders or management celebrities who promote 'stereotyped roles and scenarios' when it comes to managing organizational change. According to Evans (2004), there are four stages that affect productivity as the organization deals with change: denial, resistance, exploration, and renewal. He defines resistance as the inability of employees to accept or embrace a change that management wants to implement. He notes an equal rate of 15% among those who support and those who oppose a certain change, while the remaining 70% are 'sitting on the fence.' He further adds that such resistance could be due to frustration and anxiety, potential loss of status, payment, or power, fear of an unknown future and uncertainty of adaptability, perceived unfairness of the change, violation of mutual trust, loyalty, and commitment, a member having a competing commitment that does not fit with the change, the desire to protect what the employee perceives as the best interests of the organization, and the intention to stir debate and suggest other options. In their contribution, Thomas and Hardy (2011) add that not all forms of resistance lead to negative results, as some could even facilitate or serve as a catalyst for change. It is worth noting that some resistance to change should be expected as a norm.

In his scholarly contribution, Baker (1989) indicated that there are occasions where management decisions create situations in which normal uneasiness becomes a severe problem or a major issue within the organization. For example, a lack of information provided by managers often results in employees feeling affected or neglected. Therefore, it is important for managers to provide as much information as possible before implementing change and to further inform affected employees of the reasons for the change. Workers who receive correct and timely information about a change are better at accepting it than those who do not (Keohane, 2010). Uncertainty about new work expectations is another example: workers may resist change initiatives due to uncertainty about the new tasks they will have to perform. Anxiety increases if they are not adequately informed of the skills and knowledge required to perform these new tasks, as they fear they may lack them. According to Mohrman and Lawler (2012), it is the responsibility of managers to assure workers and other staff that the required training and knowledge will be adequately provided to enhance their performance. Fine (1986) argues that humans always resist change, even when it is related to growth and development. Hence, fear of the unknown is the primary factor that creates this resistance. Therefore, change agents, managers in charge of implementing change, or administrators must have the ability to evaluate why an employee's reaction to change escalates from simple uneasiness to negative or even aggressive behavior, such as absenteeism, boycotts, and even sabotage (Baker, 1989).

2.3.10. Attitudes and Reactions to Change

Al Shebi (2016) posits that the natural tendency for leaders is to avoid and restrict change unless it is minor and no significant damage is envisaged. He cited Watson (2011), who noted that it is very important to research why and how resistance to change develops within an organization. According to Torrington and Weightman (1994), there are four broad types of change:

- Imposition—initiated by someone else, normally from 'on high' or externally.
- Adaptation—changes in attitude or behavior at the behest of others.
- Growth—responses to opportunities, normally with favorable consequences.
- Creativity—where individuals are in control. Torrington and Weightman (1994) and Watson (2001) share a common position on the likely reactions to change:
- Enthusiastic cooperation and support, acceptance.
- Passive resignation—indifference, apathy, loss of interest, minimal contribution.
- Passive resistance—regressive behavior, non-learning behavior.
- Active resistance—protests, working to rule, minimal work, slowing down, committing errors intentionally. Any organizational change initiative often meets resistance, which Coch and French (1948: 520) describe as "a combination of individual reactions to frustration with strong group-induced forces," while Lawrence (1954) explains resistance to change as "one of the most baffling and recalcitrant problems which business executives face." Hirscheim and Newman (1988) count resistance to change as an adverse reaction, while

Nadler (1993), Pugh (1993), and Carnall (1994) view it as a problem to be solved or minimized (Zimmermann, 2011).

As previously mentioned, authors in the field agree that resistance to change is due to fear of the unknown, where team members are unable to envision the outcome of change and instead are driven by the premonition of losing their current safety and security. This phenomenon makes resistance to change commonplace in any change initiative, where it surfaces in various forms. For instance, in some cases, team members may try to derail the change initiative or slow down the entire process by adopting disruptive strategies (Durant, 1999). This, in turn, may leave organizations with only two options: either to eliminate the core source of resistance (dismissing the main protagonists of change) or to formulate counter-strategies (through discussions and campaigns) to eliminate the cause of resistance. Organizations often view resistance to change negatively, and researchers like Durant (1999) observe that the intensity of that outlook is reflected in such organizational actions (Hinds, 2003).

Resistance to change can also occur through the direct denial of a section or the entire workforce, who may refuse to accept that change is necessary for eliminating barriers to organizational sustainability and growth. For example, an organization may anticipate the possibility of losing competitive advantage due to outdated technology and business policies but may struggle to convince its workforce about the validity of this futuristic vision. In such cases, the organization would have no alternative but to continue explaining the necessity of change, with the hope that, at some point, the workforce will embrace it (Demers, 2007). Resistance to change does not end with these instances but may take even more complex forms, as observed by Durant

(1999). For example, workforce members may initially comply with change due to unspoken pressure but later become disapproving, forcing the organization to re-strategize its entire change initiative to prevent failure (Hinds, 2003). Maurer (1996) demonstrated that 50%-70% of all major corporate change efforts fail, with resistance to change identified as the main contributor (Dent, 2002). Despite extensive research on resistance to change, limitations remain. Jermier et al. (1994) argue that both the interests of managers and workers must be equally considered during the change process. Block (1993) highlighted that resistance to change might occur when employees distrust management or have had negative past experiences with change. O'Toole (1995) identified that resistance to change primarily arises from the desire to protect established social relationships and the perceived threat of losing them (Dent, 2002).

Basically, any attempt to introduce organizational change will experience some form of resistance, which could be severe in certain instances and mild in others. The main reason for resistance to change is a lack of understanding of the change process. Additionally, workers are naturally reluctant to change as they are accustomed to the existing methods of working. Another key reason is the lack of trust in the new process as opposed to the existing one. Resistance to change can be broadly analyzed on two levels: individual resistance to change and organizational resistance to change (Hinds, 2003).

There are many sources of individual resistance to change, such as habits, security, selective information processing, economic factors, and fear of the unknown. It is said that human beings are naturally creatures of habit. Numerous options and decisions must be made every day, and concern for security is another significant factor.

Generally, people are afraid of and likely to resist change because it threatens their sense of safety. For example, when Ford Australia introduced new robotic equipment, many employees expressed their dislike by refusing to use the new equipment in factories (Hellriegel and Slocum, 2009). People may also fear that change will lower their earning ability, particularly if they struggle to perform after the change process, especially when pay is closely linked to productivity (Baker, 1989). Change increases uncertainty and, in turn, heightens the fear of the unknown. This fear arises primarily due to a lack of knowledge about the change process, its objectives, and its outcomes. As a result, people tend to avoid learning about the entire change process and selectively gather only the information that is relevant to them. Selective information processing occurs when individuals make decisions based only on what they prefer (Hellriegel and Slocum, 2009). This selective approach prevents individuals from seeing the full picture, increasing their level of resistance.

According to Kübler-Ross's (1969) framework, individuals experience five main emotional responses to change: denial, resistance, acceptance, exploration, and commitment. Initially, individuals deny and reject the change process. However, once change is communicated, workers begin listening and contemplating it. After a successful training period, they accept the change and start exploring it, entering the exploration stage (Fine, 1986). Once they are fully convinced of the process, they commit to its implementation (Tozer, 2012).

According to Hellriegel and Slocum (2009), six major sources of resistance can be identified in an organizational context. Organizations have built-in systems, structures, and processes to maintain stability. When an organization undergoes change, structural inertia resists instability. Group inertia occurs when groups and teams adhere to a set of common values and beliefs. When faced with change, these groups may collectively resist to maintain their existing behaviors. Most of the time, change is an interconnected activity—no process can be changed in isolation. Many change programs fail due to a lack of focus on the process and inadequate planning. Some groups may also lose their competitive advantage due to change. For example, when technological change is introduced, mechanics and technicians in a factory might feel that their jobs are threatened. The change process can also impact existing power dynamics and decision-making authority. Naturally, workers may resist any dilution of their existing power. Furthermore, changes in the process may alter resource allocation. Once internal employee groups become accustomed to accessing certain resources, they are likely to resist any modifications (Griffin and Moorhead, 2011).

Beyond individual and organizational resistance, barriers to change can also emerge from business managers themselves. Daft (1998) described several factors that contribute to such resistance. One is an excessive focus on costs—when management prioritizes cost control, they may deliberately avoid change initiatives, fearing that these will increase the company's expenses (Griffin and Moorhead, 2011). Another factor is the failure to highlight benefits. Managers may not encourage change if they fail to recognize its long-term benefits over short-term costs. Lack of coordination and cooperation can also hinder change, as managers may perceive the process as complex and unclear. Additionally, uncertainty avoidance plays a role—managers may resist change to avoid dealing with uncertainty. Rapp et al. (2011) argue that, on an individual level, managers may be reluctant to take risks when implementing change processes.

Organizational Change Management

According to Al Shebi, a range of theories and concepts on change management has been developed by various authors, each offering different perspectives and arguments. He cited Kurt Lewin (1951), one of the most well-known scholars in organizational change management. Lewin (1951) introduced the change process in three steps (Pasmore et al., 2010):

- Unfreeze
- Change
- Refreeze
- Unfreezing

This is the most critical stage in the change process. It involves preparing an organization for change by highlighting the necessary measures to move away from the current state or comfort zones. This stage primarily aims to educate employees about the importance and necessity of change while emphasizing the consequences of failing to adapt. The goal is to reduce potential employee resistance to change. When employees are aware of the change process and understand its significance, implementing change initiatives becomes easier. Once employees adopt the right mindset for change, Lewin (1951) suggests that managers should move on to the second stage.

2.3.10.1. Change/Transition

At this stage, employees begin implementing the change measures. This is an internal process of responding to change. Once employees are mentally prepared, it becomes easier to implement the necessary change initiatives. However, this phase is also the most challenging. Despite thorough education about the change process, there is always a possibility of resistance when change is actively taking place. Therefore, managers must handle this stage with extreme care, as the success or failure of the change process heavily depends on it. Effective communication, support, and a clear demonstration of the bigger picture are crucial during this phase (Pasmore et al., 2010). Lewin (1951) further argues that managers must ensure that the driving forces for change are stronger than the restraining forces to push the change to the desired level. On the contrary, if the restraining forces are stronger, managers will struggle to achieve the intended outcomes. The Force Field Analysis is an effective tool to use during the "Unfreezing" stage to assess the overall forces for and against the change process. This analysis provides valuable insights for change planners, enabling them to develop appropriate strategies to mitigate resistance and strengthen support (Pasmore et al., 2010; Holt and Seki, 2012).

2.3.10.2. Refreezing

This final stage involves stabilizing and integrating the changes into the organization's operations. The main objective is to ensure that the business functions smoothly with the newly implemented changes. During this phase, employees develop new routines, relationships, and work patterns. Although this phase takes time, it is crucial to monitor whether employees are genuinely practicing the new changes. Even after a successful change program, some employees may revert to outdated practices. Lewin (1951) emphasized the importance of using Force Field Analysis to identify both driving and restraining forces for organizational change, ensuring that the change is sustained over the long term (Pasmore et al., 2010).

- Driving Forces: These are a set of variables that positively influence the suggested change process. Factors such as new challenges on the job, increased rewards, improved operational efficiency, enhanced effectiveness, and reduced overhead costs can be considered driving forces. It is important to note that driving forces often emerge after the successful implementation of the change process. In other words, these are positive outcomes that are expected to occur (Ageron et al., 2012).

- Restraining Forces: Restraining forces push the change process back and attempt to maintain the status quo. In other words, these factors highlight the difficulties of the change process and the convenience of staying with the existing system. Factors such as job-related anxiety, a perception that change is less stimulating, unwillingness to take risks, and fear of losing power, status, and authority are some of the restraining forces (Holt & Seki, 2012).

Peters, in his 1987 book *thriving on Chaos*, highlighted the concept of constant change. He argued that a modest-sized, semi-autonomous, and largely self-managing team should be the fundamental building block of an organization. The author believed that only organizations that embrace constant change will succeed. He maintained that this is the best way to get closer to customers by providing them with better service. One problem with this approach is that it tends to promote the notion of a "one best way" (Peters, 1988). Peters (1988) and other authors, such as Teece (2012), who support this school of thought, argue that constant change is the only constant. In certain multinational companies, senior executives are rotated every two years to prevent them from building local power bases and to encourage cultural blending.

Beer and Nohria (2000) developed a theory entitled *Change through Balancing*. The authors argue that most change initiatives have failed worldwide mainly due to a lack of focus on central elements. They further state that rushing into change results in managers immersing themselves in details and losing focus, ultimately leading to messy situations. They explain that two perspectives are available when considering organizational change (Boonstra, 2008).

Al Shebi cited Senge (1992), who introduced the concept of the *learning organization*. These organizations continuously expand their abilities to enhance capacity and cultivate a learning-oriented culture. This can only be achieved by breaking away from the traditional model of hierarchical control, authority, and bureaucracy, where top management thinks and workers act, in order to merge thinking and action at all levels. Senge further identifies five core competencies in building a learning organization (Zbar, 1994):

- Building a Shared Vision: Ensuring that people are focused on a common vision shared by the entire organization. Without a shared vision, there will be no synergy in a crisis situation. Therefore, it is essential to build shared values and beliefs within an organization.
- Personal Mastery: Encouraging individual creativity and innovation within an organization. In a learning organization, mistakes are not punished; instead, innovation is encouraged for long-term benefits.
- Working with Mental Models: Similar to personal mastery, this allows individuals the freedom to use their assumptions and take risks in doing things differently. The primary goal is to encourage organizational learning and create a culture conducive to learning.
- Team Learning: Encouraging teamwork provides a synergistic advantage over individual learning. Personal mastery must be supported and accompanied by teamwork, allowing learning to be

practiced collectively and benefiting more people in the organization.

- Systems Thinking: The organization emphasizes understanding interrelationships rather than breaking problems into small parts.

Al Shebi also referenced Kotter (1996), whose eight-step model has made a significant contribution to the field of organizational change management. This model was presented in his book *Leading Change*, where he outlined eight steps for any change initiative:

- Create urgency for change by setting appropriate and tangible goals to inspire employees to recognize the need for change.
- Form a powerful coalition by building a team of change agents with the right people, commitment, skills, and emotional balance.
- Create and establish vision and strategy, incorporating emotional and creative aspects to drive service and efficiency.
- Communicate the vision effectively to the workforce and earn their support through quality communication.
- Remove resistance to change, addressing both theoretical and practical challenges.
- Create short-term wins and highlight them as indicators of the positive impact of total change.
- Build on the change by facilitating processes that strengthen and sustain the transformation.
- Anchor the changes in corporate culture, such as recruiting appropriate employees or promoting existing talent.

Kotter segmented these steps into three phases: preparing for change, managing change, and reinforcing change. He argues that management must secure at least 75% support from the workforce for change to be successful. His model enables management to systematically achieve this through the outlined steps. Essentially, the model emphasizes forming a powerful team of change agents, using vision as a campaign tool to eliminate resistance, and showcasing short-term wins as precursors to long-term change before anchoring it within the organization (Kotter, 1996).

AL Shebi further cited Professor Moss Kanter of Harvard Business School, a famous writer on the subject of organizational change and change management. In her book *Change Masters*, she clearly complains about how modern organizations hinder entrepreneurial thinking, irrespective of how important it is to managing change in an organization. In line with the 'Excellence School' (Peters and Waterman, 1982), she emphasized the importance of employee involvement and empowerment, along with a discussion on the combination of managerial skills needed to change the culture and strategy of the organization in order to be successful in their change initiatives (Kanter, 1983). In the same work, she identifies a number of typical managerial behaviors and policies that suppress innovative employee efforts. These include:

- Regarding any idea coming from below with suspicion.
- Ensuring that people who require your approval go through several other levels of management approval prior to your approval.
- Asking departments or individuals to challenge and criticize each other's views.
- Expressing criticisms freely and withholding admiration.
- Controlling everything carefully and reducing free decision-making.

- Highlighting the identification of problems as a sign of failure.
- Asking for justification when information or questions are raised.
- However, she has also highlighted a number of ways in which organizational creativity could be encouraged. These include:
- Developing a culture that accepts change.
- Encouraging new ideas throughout the organization.
- Increasing communication and interaction between staff members.
- Tolerating failure and encouraging experimentation.
- Linking creativity and innovation with a reward structure.
- AL Shebi, in his work, also cited Hiatt (2006), who posited that effective management of the people dimension in a change management situation involves managing five drivers of change. The initials of these drivers form the acronym ADKAR, which stands for the following:
- Awareness of the need to change.
- Desire to participate in and support the change.
- Knowledge of how to change and what the change would look like.
- Ability to implement the change on a day-to-day basis.
- Reinforcement to keep the change in place.

The ADKAR model, Biech (2007) states, is based on concepts such as aligning traditional change management activities to a set goal. It was initially introduced as a tool for determining the impact of change. However, in its new form as a change model, it charts its course of action by enhancing employees' awareness of the reasons behind the proposed change. Accordingly, it sets early communication with the workforce to convince them about the value of the proposed change and to generate eagerness among them to embrace it. After achieving the desired level of workforce awareness regarding the value of the proposed change, change agents need to gauge the level of desire among the workforce by identifying any knowledge gaps regarding the necessity and benefits of the change.

According to Hiatt (2006), this step helps change agents determine the amount of knowledge required to pass on to the workforce to achieve the desired level of willingness to change. After identifying the workforce's knowledge and skill levels, change agents can proceed to evaluate employees' ability to apply their skills based on the required knowledge. Such evaluation enables them to work on key drivers such as rewards, incentives, and encouragement, which are essential to reinforce and sustain the change (Hiatt, 2006). The above description shows that the ADKAR model adopts a series of sequential and interdependent steps to eliminate the main barriers to change, such as workforce ignorance about the benefits of change. According to this model, such ignorance is the driver of workforce resistance to change.

In the process, the ADKAR model defines change in two dimensions: the business dimension (vertical axis) and the people dimension (horizontal axis). It suggests that successful change occurs when both dimensions happen simultaneously (Hiatt, 2006). The business dimension of change under this framework involves identifying a business need or opportunity, defining scopes and objectives, and designing business solutions in the form of new processes, systems, and organizational structures intended for development and implementation (Biech, 2007). The people dimension includes a series of actions under the change process that involve management, workforce, customers, and the marketplace. Altogether, the ADKAR model acts as a step-by-step support system for change leaders in achieving the desired outcome.

Greiner (1972), according to AL Shebi, introduced the 'Organizational Growth Model,' identifying organizational change through organizational growth. He argues that change is inevitable, and organizations with a long-term vision must grow to sustain their existence. Therefore, Greiner's growth model describes how organizational change is reflected through each phase of organizational growth. This model consists of six phases, and in each phase, managers must adopt different strategies for managing change and employee behavior. For example, in the initial stage, managers should encourage creativity, and in the next stage, they should guide workers in the right direction. Merson (2011) explains that within this model, Greiner identifies six types of crisis situations:

- Crisis of leadership
- Crisis of autonomy
- Crisis of control
- Crisis of red tape
- Crisis of growth
- Crisis of identity

Crisis is referred to as the main challenge that a manager should expect in each stage of growth due to organizational change. Continuing with Greiner, he further states that each of the dynamic evolutionary growth stages eventually creates a situation of revolutionary crisis when the organization's existing methods become unproductive. It is also inevitable that organizations face both revolutionary and evolutionary phases within their life cycle. The model suggests that if managers can find ways to overcome each crisis, they will unlock opportunities for growth. Failure to do so will hinder growth opportunities (Merson, 2011; Nuaimi, 2013).

It is important to note that, like any other model or framework, Greiner's growth model has both advantages and disadvantages when managing organizational change. The advantages include providing a systematic and step-by-step approach to managing change by highlighting key areas to address. It also enables managers to develop focused strategies for overcoming challenges in different change situations. Additionally, the model identifies change through organizational growth, helping managers develop appropriate growth strategies and manage change accordingly. Furthermore, it emphasizes organic growth, where profits are typically reinvested into the business, and the need for change is understood.

However, the model also has limitations. It assumes that growth happens in a linear and consistent manner, whereas various influencing factors could disrupt the smooth flow of growth. Additionally, it does not provide guidance for managing change during organizational decline (Merson, 2011).

Other authorities cited include Burke and Litwin (1992), the proponents of the Burke-Litwin Causal Model of Organizational Performance and Change (popularly known as the B-L Model), who identified 12 theoretical constructs to distinguish between an organization's culture and climate, differentiate between transformational and transactional dynamics, and specify the nature and direction of influence of organizational variables. In defense of the organization in their model, Burke (2002) argues in another study that change is seldom linear; instead, it is more often represented as an upward spiral that accounts for both regression and growth. Additionally, Anderson (2011) adds that the model is aided and complemented by previous change models, empirical studies, and practices, making it more comprehensive.

Anderson (2011), in defense of the B-L model, further states that it visibly contains several striking features. For instance, Burke and Litwin (1992) clearly differentiate between culture and organizational climate, presenting them as distinct concepts. Climate acts as an indicator of individual perceptions regarding workplace functioning, whereas culture provides a macro vision by incorporating various values and beliefs that define the broader social system surrounding the workplace. Another key feature is the model's accommodation of both transactional and transformational dynamics, positioning transformational dynamics closer to leadership factors and transactional dynamics closer to management factors. The proximity between leadership factors and the macro vision of culture suggests that the model aims to help leaders leverage culture and values, which are key drivers of intrinsic change. Similarly, the proximity between management and climate—i.e., individual and group issues—indicates that the model enables management to address climate-related concerns, which often involve transactional behavior (Burke et al., 2008).

The structural distribution of the B-L model divides the change process into two segments. Leaders are tasked with managing three key areas of change: external environment, mission and strategy, and culture, while management is responsible for structure, climate, and systems.

Al Shebi asserts that, from Burke's perspective, the B-L model acknowledges the importance of assigning leadership to drive intrinsic change among employees while management is responsible for effecting extrinsic change (Burke et al., 2008).

Referring to resistance to change, Thomson (2010) notes that Kotter and Schlesinger (1979) identified and discussed six primary methods for managing resistance:

- Education and communication: This approach is useful when resistance is caused by a lack of information or understanding. It aims to help individuals comprehend the change process and ultimately gain support. However, it can be time-consuming and may not be effective for lower-level employees.
- Participation and involvement: This method increases the likelihood of commitment to change by involving people in the process. Ideally, it follows education and communication. Its main disadvantage is that it can be excessively time-consuming.
- Facilitation and support: This approach uses techniques such as training, counseling, and group discussions. It is particularly effective when resistance stems from insecurity or adjustment difficulties.
- Negotiation and agreement: This method is applied when a group stands to lose due to change and possesses significant power to resist. While it can be useful, it may lead to high costs and encourage other groups to negotiate after witnessing concessions.
- Manipulation and co-optation: Manipulation involves providing partial or misleading information to those unwilling to accept change, while co-optation entails "buying off" key individuals resisting change by offering promotions or other incentives. The major risk with this method is potential future repercussions from the use of misleading information.
- Explicit and implicit coercion: This strategy involves using force or threats to enforce change. It may be justified when dealing with unreasonable resistance but is fraught with ethical and legal concerns.

2.3.11. The Role of Leadership in Change Management

According to Al Shebi, James Clawson (2001) emphasized that change fuels leadership, asserting that true leaders "understand, embrace, and lead change." They use communication skills, charisma, symbols, and other emotionally compelling tools to inspire and motivate others to follow them (Alvesson & Sveningsson, 2003).

O'Reilly et al. (2005) define workplace leadership as the ability of an individual in a formally assigned hierarchical role to influence a group to achieve organizational goals. Effective leadership comprises the following elements:

- Articulating the unit's vision
- Setting a strategic direction
- Defining measurable objectives based on specified strategies
- Aligning the reward system
- Motivating subordinates
- Effectively addressing resistance to change

Weber (1998) argues that a leader must understand their institution in terms of seven critical factors: strategy, structure, systems, goals, style, personnel, and skills.

O'Reilly et al. (2005) further identify several factors that influence leadership and change management, including tenure in leadership roles, effective communication, managerial and employee support, and resource allocation. These elements are crucial to ensuring a leader's success in implementing organizational change.

Alvesson and Sveningsson (2003) highlight that employee morale improves when leaders actively listen to their subordinates and treat them with respect. These daily interactions—alongside business operations, corporate rules, bureaucracy, and other organizational aspects—form a distinctive pattern unique to each institution.

This pattern, which Edgar Schein (1985) referred to as organizational culture, is transmittable, allowing new members to adopt the appropriate ways of perceiving, thinking, and feeling while working within the organization (cited in Harder, 1999). Leaders and managers must be conscious of this culture, as it significantly influences an organization's adaptability to change—a point also emphasized by Latta (2009).

The theory of transformational leadership proposed by Bass and Avolio (1994), cited in the work of Wodak et al. (2011), involves a leader's capability to communicate ideals, inspire corporate identity, provide critical insights, and consider the needs of others. Carlyle-Garrick (2006) states that the basis of trait theory emerged from the great man theory. When leaders practice leadership, critical leadership qualities are illustrated and observed by others. Therefore, people can learn from them, or individuals with these qualities could be hired. This theory also discusses the importance of having the necessary skills for a leader, along with leadership traits.

Stogdill (1974) identified leadership traits as well as the necessary skills that an effective leader should possess. Some of the main leadership traits identified by this theory include adaptability to situations, sensitivity to the environment, cooperativeness, assertiveness, decisiveness, dominance, energy, self-confidence, and the ability to manage in stressful situations. In addition, some of the most essential skills of a leader are identified as intelligence, creativity, diplomacy, organization, persuasiveness, and possession of social skills (Greenberg, 1994).

The behavioral theories of leadership include the works of several authors, including Lewin, as discussed earlier. The managerial grid developed by Blake and Mouton (1964) identifies leadership and management styles using two parameters: concern for production and concern for people and employees. Depending on the degree of priority given, they have also identified five leadership styles: country club, impoverished style, middle-of-the-road, team management, and produce-or-perish. According to the authors, the best leadership style to adopt is the team management style, where leaders give the highest concern to both production and employees. Lussier and Achua (2009) argue that the worst style to adopt is the impoverished style, as workers are not impressed by it at all.

Lewin (1939), in his work, identified three leadership styles: autocratic, democratic, and laissez-faire leadership. In the autocratic style, leaders make decisions alone without consulting subordinates. This is effective when decision-making does not require collaborative, cross-functional expertise and when the decision is unlikely to change due to subordinate input. In this style, subordinate contribution is minimal, and motivation levels are low. In the democratic style, leaders encourage subordinate participation and contribution to the decision-making process. However, the final decision is made by the leader. This style of leadership is appreciated by subordinates, as they feel their contributions are valued. One challenge with this leadership style is that decision-making may take longer due to the number of opinions and options considered.

Laissez-faire leaders provide maximum empowerment and authority to their subordinates in the decision-making process. This leadership style offers subordinates freedom in decision-making and can serve as a strong motivator for employees. However, a major disadvantage of this style is that the lack of proper monitoring of employee input may lead to inappropriate decisions (Lussier & Achua, 2009). Behavioral theories analyze how leaders generally behave in day-to-day operations. However, no two situations are the same, and one leadership style may not always help leaders succeed in different scenarios. Hence, the situational or contingency approach favors leadership that adapts to the encountered situation and explains that leaders should act according to the given circumstances (Bolden et al., 2011).

Fiedler (1967) emphasizes in his study the need for leaders to adapt their style in accordance with the situation to be managed in his contingency model. He states that different situations create different leadership requirements, and based on that, leaders must develop relevant strategies. He highlights three specific factors that define a given situation. The first is leader-member relations, which refer to the relationship between the leader and the subordinates. If the relationship is strong, it is easier to obtain subordinate support in a given situation. The second factor is task structure, which pertains to the complexity of the given task. The third is position power, which refers to the amount of power and authority given to a leader in an organization. This factor is particularly important in decision-making, as it often plays a key role in determining success.

Fiedler further states that there is no universally good or bad leadership style but rather what is appropriate in a given situation. Hence, the leadership style used depends on the leader's personality and, most importantly, the situation at hand. For example, task-oriented leaders may be best suited for sales, while relationship-oriented leaders may excel in managing customer relationships. Therefore, the leadership style to be adopted always depends on the specific context of a situation (Bolden et al., 2011).

The Blanchard model (Blanchard, 1993) also follows a situational approach to leadership. This theory considers organizational direction and the tasks to be completed in alignment with that direction, a concept referred to as task behavior. Additionally, it takes into account the type and level of relationship behavior between members and the level of maturity of subordinates. Task behavior involves leaders allocating tasks to subordinates with clear instructions for completion, reflecting one-way communication. Relationship behavior, on the other hand, is based on two-way or multi-way communication between leaders and subordinates, including listening, supporting, and facilitating.

The maturity level dimension assesses a leader's confidence in an individual subordinate's ability to complete given tasks with minimal supervision. This assessment depends on factors such as task complexity, prior experience, local support, and other relevant aspects. In summary, a leader's behavior can be categorized into two broad sections: directive behavior and supportive behavior. Directive behavior is based on one-way communication and is typically associated with autocratic management styles, where subordinates follow strict instructions. Supportive behavior, on the other hand, fosters open communication, employee empowerment, and the necessary support for task completion.

Shrinberg (2010) concurs and adds that based on these two variables, four leadership paradigms have emerged: delegation, supporting, coaching, and directing. Nicholson (2009) explains that transactional leadership is a style based on setting clear objectives and goals, as well as using punishments and rewards to encourage compliance. Lussier and Achua (2004) state that researchers regard this style as one that promotes stability, aiming to maintain consistency through regular economic and social exchanges rather than encouraging change.

Bryant (2003) highlights three distinctive features of this style. First, transactional leaders formulate a common organizational goal with their followers. Second, they offer rewards or promises of rewards to motivate performance.

Third, they respond to the immediate self-interests of workers during the process of achieving the goal. However, a number of researchers (Barnett et al., 2001; Gellis, 2001; Jung & Avolio, 1999) observe that this model, which uses both rewards and punishments through extrinsic incentives like money or gifts, is prone to exploitation of the reward system for the benefit of leaders.

Brown and Moshavi (2002) further argue that the individual goals of leaders and followers under this style tend to diverge. Since this leadership style encourages both leaders and followers to maximize material gains, they may exploit all available opportunities, such as rank and job specifications, to their advantage. This observation suggests that money and rank are the primary drivers of transactional leadership, where followers comply in exchange for incentives.

2.3.11.1. Gap in Knowledge

From the foregoing review of the literature by various authorities cited, who have made immense contributions to the subject of leadership in crisis situations, particularly in leading organizational change during a recession, it is evident that most of the prescriptions or panaceas for change are reactionary rather than proactive. They are curative rather than preventive. The researcher has identified a gap in knowledge, which has evidently opened a chapter of opportunity for further research in this field. This research will focus on leadership structures designed to foresee and prevent organizational crises during a recession, ensuring that such organizations not only survive but exceed their targets even in turbulent times.

2.4. Summary of Literature Review

This research is based on three leadership theories that form the framework for this thesis. These theories are the contingency or situational theory of leadership, the behavioral theory of leadership, and the trait theory of leadership.

The conceptual review focused on three key concepts: leadership, organizational change, and recession. An in-depth study of several sources was conducted to examine the various variables related to these three key concepts.

The empirical review involved an extensive study of the literature to explore the subject of recession and its impact on both profit and nonprofit organizations. The researcher further reviewed literature on the dynamics of organizational change, covering areas such as change strategy, change management, resistance to change, and the role of leadership in enforcing organizational change, particularly during a recession.

Chapter 3 | Research Methodology

This chapter presents the research methods adopted in this work.

3.1. Research Design

A wide range of methods are used in research. These methods vary depending on the sources of information being gathered, how the information is sampled, and the types of instruments used in data collection (Baridam, 2001). For the purpose of this work, the method adopted is descriptive survey research. It is also a cross-sectional study that focused on the post-COVID-19 recession from April 2020 to March 2021. It is a qualitative study that sought to describe the role of leadership in organizational change during the post-COVID-19 recession.

3.2. Population for the Study

Chisnol (1981) asserted that the population is the total number of individuals relevant to a particular survey. It refers to the totality of all elements that possess a common characteristic within a given geographical location. According to Okeke (1995), the population is the collection of elements, units, or individuals for which information is sought. The population studied by the researcher comprised nine organizations in Port Harcourt, Rivers State. These organizations are:

i. Firstlove Assembly, Port Harcourt
ii. Jevinik Restaurant, Port Harcourt
iii. Rehoboth Health & Emergency Response, Port Harcourt
iv. TechnipFMC, Port Harcourt
v. MPraise Yoghurts, Port Harcourt
vi. Sterling Bank, Rumuola Branch, Port Harcourt

vii. International Health Management Services, Port Harcourt
viii. Total Nigeria PLC, Port Harcourt
ix. Rivers State Ministry of Works, Port Harcourt
x. Linus Ochai Foundation

3.3. Sample Size and Sampling Technique

This is a proportion of the population taken as a representation of the entire population. It is within this proportion that facts are gathered, analyzed, and a logical conclusion is drawn.

The sample size for this research work comprised a total of ten profit and non-profit organizations. Questionnaires were randomly distributed to ten management staff in leadership positions in the selected organizations. The survey was carried out on a sample of respondents randomly selected from the study population, and primary data were collected. The method of selection was the simple random sampling technique.

3.4. Nature/Sources of Data

This research work utilized both primary and secondary data. The primary data for the study was sourced through the administration of a structured questionnaire. The secondary data for this study was obtained from related published works on the subject of leading organizational change in a recession. The questionnaire is considered a well-recognized and convenient tool for data generation (Bryman & Bell, 2003). The administered questionnaire was structured with open-ended questions, allowing respondents to answer independently.

The questionnaire for this study comprised two main sections. The demographic section focused on items of demographic nature, such as name, gender, qualification, marital status, and designation. The second section focused on questions derived from the variables in this study. The researcher adopted a four-scale approach in the questionnaire design. The scale utilized was: IA = I Agree, ISA = I Strongly Agree, ID = I Disagree, and ISD = I Strongly Disagree.

3.5. Methods of Data Collection/Instrument

As stated earlier, this research work is descriptive and, as such, attempted to describe the role of leadership in ensuring organizational change during a recession. According to Eketu (2009), concepts are measured in their abstract forms, operationalized through clearly stated indicators expressing manifest properties that can be observed, experienced, and described.

The researcher personally distributed the questionnaires randomly to ten management staff in leadership positions in the selected organizations. A total of 90 questionnaires were distributed to respondents. A total of 67 respondents answered the questions and returned the questionnaires, indicating approximately 75% cooperation from respondents. The key instrument used for data collection was the structured questionnaire, which contained questions aligned with three core concepts: Leadership, Organizational Change, and Recession.

The concept of leadership was operationalized using five dimensions: influence, problem-solving skills, effective communication, emotional intelligence, and commitment. The concept of organizational change was operationalized using four dimensions: creativity, innovation, adaptation, and modification. Finally, the concept of recession was operationalized with the following dimensions: high unemployment, a decline in income, increased poverty, and high government borrowing.

3.6. Validity of Instrument

In this study, construct validity (discriminant and convergent) was utilized. Kothari (2004) described construct validity as an assessment of the correlation levels between the measures of a variable (convergent) and the extent to which it varies or does not correlate with the measures of another variable (discriminant). While construct validity is considered a strong indicator of measurement preciseness and relatedness, it is an intra-rater form of assessment and does not provide pre-empirical validation of the instrument itself. Hence, this study adopted content validity, which, as described by Sarantakos (2005), draws on existing theoretical and operational domains of variables in their measurements. Thus, all instrument items for this study were adopted from existing theoretical and operational definitions or empirical research conducted in previous studies.

3.7. Reliability of Instrument

Reliability is an essential determinant used to assess the consistency of a measure. A measure is considered reliable if it produces consistent results (Neil, 2009). Furthermore, reliability for this study was tested using the Cronbach alpha (1951) reliability test. As an intra-rater test, the Cronbach alpha assesses data consistency and indicates the reliability of the instrument concerning clarity, replicability, and data consistency. Neuman (2006) noted that the Cronbach alpha is one of the most popular and widely accepted reliability tests in social, management, and behavioral sciences. A test result of 0.70 or above is considered an acceptable reliability value (Nunally, 1970). Given its popularity among social researchers, this study adopted the Nunally (1970) threshold of 0.70.

3.8. Administration of Instrument

The researcher personally administered 100 copies of the questionnaires to respondents (senior managers with leadership roles in the nine selected organizations). The structured questionnaires were directly administered by the researcher and retrieved for eventual analysis of the collected data. The study focused on distributing questionnaires to ten top management staff in ten organizations in Port Harcourt. While 100 questionnaires were distributed, 90 were successfully retrieved.

3.9. Methods of Data Analysis

The data are presented in tables as frequency distributions. In the analysis, the techniques of percentage and frequency are applied.

The data generated for this study included demographic data as well as data on the target variables collected through questionnaires, coupled with the Statistical Package for the Social Sciences (SPSS) version 22. Furthermore, the analysis was conducted at the demographic, primary, and secondary stages.

3.9.1. Demographic Data Analysis

The demographic data for this study were analyzed using descriptive tools such as simple percentages and frequency distributions. Contingency tables were utilized to illustrate the distribution of each variable.

3.9.2. Primary Stage of Analysis

The primary stage involved assessing the distributions of responses and evaluating the overall levels of manifestation of the variables within the contexts specified in the study. Measures of central tendency (e.g., mean) and dispersion (e.g., standard deviation) were utilized to assess average responses and experiences of the variables within the specified contexts.

3.9.3. Secondary Stage of Analysis

The secondary stage of analysis involved testing the study's hypotheses. Tests were conducted using Spearman's rank-order correlation coefficient at a 0.05 level of significance, based on a 95% confidence interval. The choice of Spearman's rank-order correlation was based on its flexibility in assessing data scaled on both ordinal and interval scales (Sarantakos, 2005; Sullivan, 2001). Additionally, Spearman's correlation is a non-parametric test, meaning it makes no assumptions about data distributions (e.g., normality of distributions, homogeneity of variance), making it a reliable choice for testing correlations in management and social sciences research (Sullivan, 2001).

3.9.4. Decision Rule

The decision rule for accepting or rejecting hypotheses was based on the adoption of a probability value as the threshold, with the critical region defined as $P < 0.05$ and $P > 0.05$. Therefore, when $P < 0.05$, the null hypothesis was considered false and rejected (indicating significant relationships), whereas when $P > 0.05$, the null hypothesis was considered true and accepted (indicating insignificant relationships).

3.9.5. Summary

In summary, mean scores determined the acceptance or rejection of rating items, standard deviation, frequencies, and percentages were used, Spearman's rank-order correlation established relationships between variables, and descriptive statistics were used to analyze the questionnaires.

Chapter 4 | Data Presentation, Analysis, and Interpretation

This chapter presents the data collected and attempts to analyze them using the descriptive method of data analysis. According to Lindlof (2010), this method organizes collected data in a way that describes the nature and type of data collected. This can be achieved using various diagrams and tables. For the purpose of this work, tables have been presented for analysis.

4.1. Administration of Questionnaire

4.1.1. Fieldwork

The results of the fieldwork are presented in this subsection of the chapter. The results herein address data retrieved through the distribution of structured questionnaire copies. A total of 100 questionnaire copies were distributed to the target agencies, out of which only 90 copies were successfully retrieved. Based on cross-checks and error assessments, all 90 copies were considered valid and useful for the study's analysis. This indicates a 90% questionnaire retrieval rate. The details of the distribution and retrieval are presented below:

S/No	Status of Questionnaires	Number of Questionnaires	Percentage
1	Distributed	100	100%
2	Retrieved	90	90%
3	Not Retrieved	10	10%
4	Discarded	Nil	0%
5	Analyzed	90	10%

Table I: Breakdown of Total Questionnaires Distributed, Retrieved and Analyzed

4.1.2. Demographic Analysis

This section of the study presents the analysis of demographic variables. The tools adopted in this section include frequency and simple percentage statistical tools. Results are illustrated using contingency tables for each item.

S/No	Sex	Number	Percentage
1	Male	70	77.78%
2	Female	20	22.22%
3	Total	90	100%

Table II: Gender Distribution of Respondents

The table above presents the gender distribution of respondents. A total of 70 males, representing 77.78% of the respondents, received and responded to the questionnaire, while 20 females, representing 22.22%, also participated in the research. Inferentially, the organizations under study provide opportunities for women to pursue careers in leadership positions without gender discrimination.

Category	Frequency	Percentage
26-30	20	22.22%
31-35	10	11.1%
36-40	10	11.1%
41 ABOVE	50	55.56%
TOTAL	90	100%

Table III: Age Distribution of Respondents

The data above show that respondents aged 26-30 account for 22.22%, those aged 31-35 account for 11.1%, those aged 36-40 account for 11.1%, while those aged 41 and above account for 55.56%. The inference drawn from this data suggests a mix of both younger and middle-aged individuals. This blend facilitates knowledge sharing, mentoring, and succession planning.

Category	Frequency	Percentage
Single	28	31.1%
Married	37	41.1%
Widowed	14	15.5%
Divorced	6	6.6%
Separated	5	5.56%
Total	90	100%

Table IV: Distribution of Respondents According To Marital Status

From the data in Table 4, 28 respondents (31.1%) were single, 37 (41.1%) were married, 14 (15.5%) were widowed, 6 (6.6%) were divorced, and 5 (5.56%) were separated. The researcher infers that a significant percentage of those in leadership positions are married, suggesting that their marital experiences may contribute to problem-solving within their organizations. Additionally, the high percentage of married leaders may indicate that their emotional intelligence fosters organizational stability.

Category	Frequency	Percentage
Ssce	NIL	0%
Ond	NIL	0%
Hnd	25	27.78%
Bachelor	40	44.4%
Masters	25	27.78%
Other Professional Qualifications	-	0%
Total	90	100%

Table V: Distribution of Respondents According to Educational Qualification

As indicated in Table 5, there were no respondents with a Senior Secondary School Certificate (SSCE) or an Ordinary National Diploma (OND). A total of 25 respondents (27.78%) had a Higher National Diploma (HND), 40 respondents (44.4%) had a Bachelor's degree, and 25 respondents (27.78%) had a Master's degree. These results reveal that all respondents possess the educational qualifications necessary to provide effective leadership solutions.

Category	Frequency	Percentage
Chief Executive Officers (Ceo)	15	16.6%
Managing Directors	20	22.22%
Senior Managers	30	33.3%
Mid-Level Managers	14	15.5%
Junior Managers	11	12.2%
Total	90	100%

Table VI: Distribution According to Position

Table 6 indicates that 15 respondents (16.6%) were Chief Executive Officers (CEOs), 20 respondents (22.22%) were Managing Directors, 30 respondents (33.3%) were Senior Managers, 14 respondents (15.5%) were Mid-Level Managers, and 11 respondents (12.2%) were Junior Managers. The researcher infers that nearly all respondents hold leadership positions that have a significant impact on the health of their respective organizations.

4.2. Data Analysis and Results

Univariate Section In this section of the study, the data distribution for the variables is presented. The distribution covers the three main variables of the study: Leadership, Organizational Change, and Recession. Each variable is assessed based on the distributions of their dimensions/measures and the corresponding distributions for their indicators. The mean and standard deviation are utilized in this section to ascertain the direction of opinions as well as the extent of those opinions based on the scale (4-point) adopted in the study. A base mean of $x = 2.5$ is adopted, where interpretations for scales follow "affirm" (where $x > 2.5$) and "non-affirm" (where $x < 2.5$) summarized rating response.

Leadership: This is the predictor variable in the study. It is assessed based on the instrument that examines the extent to which the participants consider the influence, problem-solving skills, effective communication, commitment, and emotional intelligence of leadership in their various organizations, as well as the impact on organizational change during a recession.

Organizational Change: This is the criterion variable in the study. It is assessed based on the instrument that examines the extent to which the participants consider their organizations' chances of survival in the face of recession, particularly the post-COVID-19 recession. A total of four measures—creativity, innovation, adaptation, and modification—were considered while measuring organizational survival. The researcher has carried out a univariate analysis of the various variables.

Recession: The third variable in this study is Recession. The analysis in this section assessed the extent to which recession was mitigated in various organizations due to the efforts of leadership in effecting changes in the organization. Four dimensions were considered: unemployment, fall in income, rise in poverty, and high government borrowing. With the aid of the research instrument, the researcher has conducted a univariate analysis of the variables.

"Your leadership style influences team members to attain organizational goals during the post-COVID-19 recession."

Category	Frequency	Percentage
Agree	45	50%
Strongly Agree	21	23.3%
Disagree	15	16.6%
Strongly Disagree	9	10%
Total	90	100%

Table VII: Distribution of Respondents to the Question

From the data in Table VII, 45 respondents agree that the leadership style of the leader influences team members to attain organizational goals. This represents 50% of the total respondents. Twenty-one respondents strongly agree, accounting for 23.3%, while 15 respondents disagree (16.6%), and 9 respondents strongly disagree (10%).

Category	Frequency	Percentage
Agree	56	62%
Strongly Agree	24	26.6%
Disagree	6	6.6%
Strongly Disagree	4	4.4%
Total	90	100%

Table VIII: Distribution of Respondents to the Question: "Your leadership style plays a crucial role in the completion of tasks allocated to each member of your team during the recession."

The data in Table VIII shows that 56 respondents agree with the question, accounting for 62%. Twenty-four respondents strongly agree (26.6%), while 6 respondents disagree (6.6%), and 4 respondents strongly disagree (4.4%).

Category	Frequency	Percentage
Agree	32	35.5%
Strongly Agree	43	47.78%
Disagree	9	10%
Strongly Disagree	6	6.6%
Total	90	100%

Table IX: Distribution of Respondents on the Question: "Your leadership style allows room for team members to innovate with the aim of contributing to organizational growth during the recession."

The data in table IX reveals that 32 respondents agree to the question, accounting for 35.5%. 43 The data in Table IX reveals that 32 respondents agree with the question, accounting for 35.5%. Forty-three respondents strongly agree (47.78%), while 9 respondents disagree (10%) and 6 respondents strongly disagree (6.6%).

Category	Frequency	Percentage
Agree	36	40%
Strongly Agree	44	48.8%
Disagree	6	6.6%
Strongly Disagree	4	4.4%
Total	90	100%

Table X: Distribution of Respondents on the Question: "Your Leadership Style to a Great Extent Encourages Teamwork During The Recession."

The data in Table X reveals that 36 respondents agree (40%), 44 respondents strongly agree (48.8%), while 6 respondents disagree (6.6%) and 4 respondents strongly disagree (4.4%).

Category	Frequency	Percentage
Agree	37	41.1%
Strongly Agree	53	58.8%
Disagree	NIL	0%
Strongly Disagree	NIL	0%
Total	90	100%

Table XI: Distribution of Respondents on the Question: "Your Emotional Intelligence Skill Prevents Crises Between You And Team Members During The Recession."

The data in Table XI reveals that 37 respondents agree (41.1%), and 53 respondents strongly agree (58.8%). No respondents disagreed or strongly disagreed.

Category	Frequency	Percentage
Agree	46	51.1%
Strongly Agree	36	40%
Disagree	8	8.8%
Strongly Disagree	Nil	0%
Total	90	100%

Table XII: Distribution of Respondents on the Question: "Your Emotional Intelligence Skill Averts Crises Among Team Members During The Recession."

The data in Table XII shows that 46 respondents agree (51.1%), while 36 respondents strongly agree (40%), and 8 respondents disagree (8.8%). No respondents strongly disagreed.

Category	Frequency	Percentage
Agree	26	28.6%
Strongly Agree	24	26.6%
Disagree	33	36.67%
Strongly Disagree	7	7.78%
Total	90	100%

Table XIII: Distribution of Respondents on the Question: Some Contingencies or Situations beyond Your Control in the Environment Negatively Impacted Your Leadership and the Growth of Your Organization During The Recession

The data in Table XIII shows that 26 respondents agree with the question, accounting for 28.6%, while 24 respondents strongly agree. Additionally, 33 respondents disagree, accounting for 36.67%, while 7 respondents strongly disagree.

Category	Frequency	Percentage
Agree	24	26.6%
Strongly Agree	56	62.2%
Disagree	4	4.4%
Strongly Disagree	6	6.6%
Total	90	100%

Table XIV: Distribution of Respondents on the Question: Your problem-solving skills as a leader contributed to organizational profit and economic stability during the recession.

The data in Table XIV shows that 24 respondents agree, accounting for 26.6%, while 56 respondents strongly agree, accounting for 62.2%. Additionally, 4 respondents disagree, accounting for 4.4%, while 6 respondents strongly disagree, accounting for 6.6% of the total respondents.

Category	Frequency	Percentage
Agree	46	51.1%
Strongly Agree	44	48.9%
Disagree	NIL	0%
Strongly Disagree	NIL	0%
Total	90	100%

Table XV: Distribution of Respondents on the Question: Having Effective Communication Skills Enabled You to Communicate Roles to Team Members in a Clear and Concise Manner during the Recession

The data in Table XV shows that 46 respondents agree, accounting for 51.1%, while 44 respondents strongly agree, accounting for 48.9%. No respondent disagreed or strongly disagreed.

Category	Frequency	Percentage
Agree	45	50%
Strongly Agree	45	50%
Disagree	Nil	0%
Strongly Disagree	Nil	0%
Total	90	100%

Table XVI: Distribution of Respondents on the Question: As a Leader, You Were Able To Inspire Your Team Members to Be Committed to the Execution of Their Tasks during the Recession

The data in Table XVI shows that 45 respondents agree, while another 45 respondents strongly agree, accounting for 50% each. No respondents disagreed or strongly disagreed.

Category	Frequency	Percentage
Agree	37	41.1%
Strongly Agree	50	55.56%
Disagree	2	2.2%
Strongly Disagree	1	1.1%
Total	90	100%

Table XVII: Distribution of Respondents on the Question: Your Leadership Is Relational and Allows Room for Team Members' Creativity to Thrive during the Recession

The data in Table XVII shows that 37 respondents agree with the question, accounting for 41.1%. Additionally, 50 respondents strongly agree, accounting for 55.56%. Meanwhile, 2 respondents disagree, accounting for 2.2%, while 1 respondent strongly disagrees, accounting for 1.1%.

Category	Frequency	Percentage
Agree	45	50%
Strongly Agree	38	42.2%
Disagree	3	2.7%
Strongly Disagree	4	4.4%
Total	90	100%

Table XVIII: Distribution of Respondents on the Question: Your Leadership Appraises the Performance of Team Members and Rewards High Performers during the Recession

From the data in Table XVIII, it is evident that 45 respondents agree with the question, representing 50%. Additionally, 38 respondents strongly agree, representing 42.2%. Meanwhile, 3 respondents disagree, representing 2.7%, while 4 respondents strongly disagree, representing 4.4% of the total respondents.

Category	Frequency	Percentage
Agree	35	38.89%
Strongly Agree	38	42.2%
Disagree	15	16.67%
Strongly Disagree	2	2.2%
Total	90	100%

Table XVIIII: Distribution of Respondents on the Question: Your Leadership Provides Incentives to Motivate the Workforce to Remain with the Organization and Prevent a High Rate of Worker Turnover during the Recession

The data from Table XVIIII shows that 35 respondents agree, accounting for 38.89% of the respondents. Additionally, 38 respondents strongly agree, representing 42.2%. Meanwhile, 15 respondents disagree, making up 16.67%, while 2 respondents strongly disagree, accounting for 2.2% of the total respondents.

Category	Frequency	Percentage
Agree	45	50%
Strongly Agree	40	44.4%
Disagree	5	5.5%
Strongly Disagree	Nil	0%
Total	90	100%

Table XX: Distribution of Respondents on the Question: Your Creativity and Innovation as a Leader Help You Reposition Your Organization and Minimize the Impact of the Recession

Table XX shows that 45 respondents agree, accounting for 50% of the respondents. Additionally, 40 respondents strongly agree, representing 44.4%. Meanwhile, 5 respondents disagree, making up 5.5%. No respondents strongly disagreed with the question.

Category	Frequency	Percentage
Agree	51	56.6%
Strongly Agree	33	36.67%
Disagree	4	4.4%
Strongly Disagree	2	2.2%
Total	90	100%

Table XXI: Distribution of Respondents on the Question: Under Your Leadership, a Culture of Innovation and Creativity Is Encouraged and Celebrated Among Team Members during the Recession

The data in Table XXI shows that 51 respondents agree, representing 56.6%, while 33 respondents strongly agree, representing 36.67%. On the other hand, 4 respondents disagree, accounting for 4.4%, and 2 respondents strongly disagree, making up 2.2%.

Category	Frequency	Percentage
Agree	40	44.4%
Strongly Agree	45	50%
Disagree	3	2.7%
Strongly Disagree	2	2.2%
Total	90	100%

Table XXII: Distribution of Respondents on the Question: A Transformational Leadership Style Helps Your Organization Minimize Losses and Maximize Profit during the Recession

The data in Table XXII shows that 40 respondents agree, accounting for 44.4%, while 45 respondents strongly agree, representing 50%. Meanwhile, 3 respondents disagree, making up 2.7%, and 2 respondents strongly disagree, accounting for 2.2% of the total respondents.

Category	Frequency	Percentage
Agree	50	55.56%
Strongly Agree	40	44.4%
Disagree	Nil	16.7%
Strongly Disagree	Nil	0%
Total	90	100%

Table XXIII: Distribution of Respondents on the Question: Your Leadership Is Transformational and Serves as a Great Source of Motivation for Team Members during the Recession

The data in Table XXIII shows that 50 respondents agree, accounting for 55.56%, while 40 respondents strongly agree, representing 44.4%. No respondents disagreed or strongly disagreed.

Category	Frequency	Percentage
Agree	35	38.89%
Strongly Agree	35	38.89%
Disagree	16	17.78%
Strongly Disagree	4	4.4%
Total	90	100%

Table XXIV: Distribution of Respondents on the Question: Team Members Were Able to Innovate to Navigate the Recession Because Your Leadership Fostered a Culture of Innovation during the Recession

The data in Table XXIV shows that 35 respondents agree, accounting for 38.89%, while another 35 respondents strongly agree, representing 38.89%. Meanwhile, 16 respondents disagree, making up 17.78%, and 4 respondents strongly disagree, accounting for 4.4%.

Category	Frequency	Percentage
Agree	24	26.67%
Strongly Agree	56	62.2%
Disagree	4	4.4%
Strongly Disagree	6	6.67%
Total	90	100%

Table XXV: Distribution of Respondents on the Question: As a Leader, You Adapted and Inspired Your Team Members to Adapt to Working from Home during the Recession

The data in Table XXV shows that 24 respondents agree, accounting for 26.67%, while 56 respondents strongly agree, representing 62.2%. Meanwhile, 4 respondents disagree, making up 4.4%, and 6 respondents strongly disagree, accounting for 6.67%.

Category	Frequency	Percentage
Agree	45	50%
Strongly Agree	45	50%
Disagree	Nil	0%
Strongly Disagree	Nil	0%
Total	90	100%

Table Xxvi: Distribution of Respondents on the Question: Modifying the Organizational Structure during the Recession Motivated Team Members to Adhere to the Discipline of Completing Tasks According to Schedule

The data in Table XXVI shows that 45 respondents agree, accounting for 50%, while another 45 respondents strongly agree, also representing 50%. No respondents disagreed or strongly disagreed.

Category	Frequency	Percentage
Agree	26	28.89%
Strongly Agree	39	43.3%
Disagree	21	23.3%
Strongly Disagree	4	4.4%
Total	90	100%

Table XXVI: Distribution of Respondents on the Question There Was an Intentional Effort to Sensitive the Workforce to Embrace New Structures and New Strategies for Task Execution during the Recession

From the data in table XXVI, 26 respondents agree, accounting for 28.89%; 39 respondents strongly disagree, accounting for 43.3%. 21 respondents disagree, accounting for 23.35 of respondents while 4 respondents strongly disagree, accounting for 4.4% of respondents.

4.2.1. Bivariate Section

According to Kothari (2004), when there is a correlation between two variables, it is considered a bivariate population, and a correlation technique should be used for such analysis. When there is a cause-and-effect relationship between one variable on one side and two or more variables on the other, it is classified as a multivariate population.

This section of the study examines the significance of the relationship between Leadership, Organizational Change, and Recession. The results of the hypothesis tests assess the relationship between the dimensions of Leadership (influence, problem-solving skills, effective communication, emotional intelligence, and commitment) and Organizational Change (creativity, innovation, adaptation, and modification), as well as their potential impact on resilience during a recession. This is reflected in the relationships stated in the hypotheses:

4.2.2. Hypotheses

- Ho1: There is no significant relationship between the influence of an organizational leader on their team members and recession.
- Ho2: There is no significant relationship between an organizational leader's problem-solving skills and recession.
- Ho3: There is no significant relationship between an organizational leader's effective communication skills and recession.
- Ho4: There is no significant relationship between an organizational leader's emotional intelligence skills and recession.
- Ho5: There is no significant relationship between an organizational leader's commitment and recession.
- Ho6: There is no significant relationship between an organizational leader's creativity and recession.
- Ho7: There is no significant relationship between an organizational leader's innovation and recession.
- Ho8: There is no significant relationship between an organizational leader's ability to adapt to change and recession.
- Ho9: There is no significant relationship between an organizational leader's ability to modify existing organizational structures and recession.

4.3. Summary of Findings

Hypotheses	Result
Ho1: There is no significant relationship between the influence of an organizational leader on his/her team members and recession.	+ve REJECTED
HO2: There is no significant relationship between the organizational leader's problem solving skill and recession.	+ve REJECTED
HO3: There is no significant relationship between the organizational leader's effective communication skill and recession.	+ve REJECTED
HO4: There is no significant relationship between the organizational leader's emotional intelligence skills and recession.	+ve REJECTED
HO5: There is no significant relationship between the organizational leader's commitment and recession.	+ve REJECTED
HO6: There is no significant relationship between the organizational leader's creativity and recession.	+ve REJECTED
HO7: There is no significant relationship between the organizational leader's innovation and recession.	+ve REJECTED
HO8: There is no significant relationship between the organizational leader's ability to adapt to change and recession.	+ve REJECTED
HO9: There is no significant relationship between the organizational leader's ability to modify existing organizational structures and recession.	+ve REJECTED

4.4. Discussion of Findings

Findings from the data collected and analyzed in this research indicate that the leadership style of a leader during a recession determines the success of an organization. Since maintaining the status quo is not an option in a recession, the leader is compelled to adopt a blend of leadership styles, ranging from authoritarian and relational to servant leadership.

The findings also revealed that the leader's emotional makeup plays a crucial role in rallying the support of team members to achieve set targets, particularly given the intense pressure that comes with a recession.

The research further discovered that customer satisfaction and loyalty can be positively influenced by the innovation, creativity, and flexibility of both the leader and team members during a recession. Creativity and innovation can turn around an organization's fortunes, even in challenging times.

Effective communication between the leader and team members, along with adequate feedback from customers, can enhance an organization's success during a recession.

From my findings, organizations that have successfully navigated and outlasted recessions have consistently been led by transformational leaders with a strong inclination for innovation and creativity.

Additional findings highlight the challenges organizations face during a recession. These challenges include poor customer patronage, dwindling revenue, and low returns on investment. In a recession, many organizations struggle to maximize profits because customers' purchasing power is significantly reduced.

Most organizations respond by downsizing and cutting costs to avoid going out of business. However, organizations with strong and dynamic leadership not only survive but thrive, remaining relevant, achieving sales, and meeting organizational goals.

Chapter 5 | Summary, Conclusions, Recommendations and Contribution to Scholarship

5.1. Summary

This study investigated the relationship between the role of character and competent leadership in steering the ship of an organization in a recessed economy. The researcher examined the characteristics of a recessed economy, particularly poor patronage of goods and services due to dwindling purchasing power of the average customer, unemployment, and rising poverty. Reports from data collected from ten organizations in Port Harcourt, Nigeria, indicate that the role of effective leadership in organizations during periods of recession cannot be overemphasized. The relationship between the concept of leadership, organizational change, and recession was measured using various empirical techniques. These techniques addressed the extent to which dimensions of leadership (influence, commitment, emotional intelligence, problem-solving skills) and dimensions of organizational change (innovation, creativity, adaptation, and modification) mitigate the dimensions of recession (high government borrowing, unemployment, low purchasing power, and poverty). All nine hypotheses tested in the study were bivariate. All nine hypotheses were rejected as the evidence from the analysis revealed that all dimensions of leadership were significantly associated with the measures of organizational change in controlling the variables of recession within the organizations represented in this study. Furthermore, leadership was observed to significantly moderate the relationship between recession and organizational change in the study population.

As such, all hypotheses were rejected based on the evidence presented by the analysis.

5.2. Conclusions

This research has provided an overview and a robust discussion on the concepts of leading organizational change in a recession, focusing on ten profit and nonprofit organizations in Port Harcourt, Nigeria. It primarily explored the perspectives of chief executive officers, managing directors, and senior and mid-level managers regarding the role of leadership in effecting organizational changes that would guarantee survival in a recession.

The researcher concludes from the data analyzed that effective leadership determines organizational change and survival in the post-COVID-19 recession. It is also evident that efficient leadership enables organizations to navigate the hurdles of a recessed economy. Transformational leadership that is dynamic, innovative, and creative, as exemplified by Singapore, forms the fulcrum for organizational and societal transformation in the face of recession and other crises.

Our empirical findings provide several important practical leadership imperatives that impact organizations, ensuring the necessary change dynamics to mitigate the effects of recession on the organizations under consideration as well as the economy. This study reveals that leaders are critical in determining the fate of organizations both in normal times and during crises. It is equally evident from this study that the attitude of a leader is as important as leadership style and other leadership competencies. Leaders, therefore, should strive to improve their creativity and innovation by providing adequate solutions that ensure stability, minimize losses, and maximize profit for their organizations.

To ensure succession and position future leaders who are better equipped to manage future crises, the current generation of leaders must be intentional about knowledge transfer. Organizational leaders should implement training programs that regularly build and improve the leadership capacity of their subordinates. Deliberate efforts should be made to close the knowledge gap between senior and junior managers.

The emotional intelligence of leaders is paramount in minimizing regular worker turnover. To prevent the loss of trained personnel, leaders should treat team members with respect and dignity. In addition to offering the necessary respect that enables employees to thrive emotionally within the organization, it is also important to establish an objective reward system based on performance appraisal. Leaders must understand that the greatest asset of any organization is its human resources. Without them, the organization will grind to a halt. Therefore, employees need encouragement and motivation to align with change rather than resist it.

This research finding emphasizes that the leadership of both profit and nonprofit organizations plays a crucial role in fostering a culture of innovation, creativity, efficiency, and commitment among team members to achieve organizational goals. Leadership must intentionally create an environment conducive to teamwork.

The research also revealed that a combination of leadership styles, including servant leadership, transformational leadership, autocratic leadership, and relational leadership, is essential to successfully navigating an organization through difficult times.

Studies have emphasized the significant correlation between leadership and organizational change. This study revealed that beyond developing and deploying a change template within an organization, effectively communicating the change process to all stakeholders and allowing them to take ownership is critical in preventing resistance to change, no matter how well-intended.

The findings of this study demonstrate that transformational leadership is the sine qua non for organizational change and survival during a recession, as evidenced by the data collected and analyzed. With the right leadership, recession and other environmental shocks that negatively impact organizational survival can be largely mitigated.

5.3. Recommendations

The following recommendations are premised on the conclusions of the study and are structured to emphasize the importance of leadership in ensuring the necessary changes that organizations must undergo to survive a recession.

a) Organizations should prioritize training and capacity building for all managers to enhance their leadership skills, particularly in problem-solving. Leaders should be educated on the importance of adopting leadership styles that provide a competitive advantage in both normal and crisis situations. The status quo cannot be maintained in a recession; therefore, leaders should blend various leadership styles, including authoritarian, relational, and servant leadership, to achieve organizational goals.

b) Greater emphasis should be placed on leadership studies to encourage leaders to reinvent themselves emotionally. The emotional health of a leader significantly influences the organizational atmosphere, which, in turn, affects team members' ability to perform efficiently. A leader's emotional resilience plays a critical role in rallying team support to meet set targets, particularly under the pressures of a recession.

c) Organizational leaders should take proactive measures to prioritize excellent service delivery, customer satisfaction, and loyalty. These can be positively influenced by the innovation, creativity, and flexibility of leaders and team members during a recession.

d) Organizations should intentionally focus on fostering creativity and innovation among leaders to turn around their fortunes, even in challenging times.

e) Organizational communication should be improved to ensure honest and effective feedback. All bottlenecks that hinder communication should be addressed. The organizational structure should serve the people, enabling them to carry out their tasks efficiently, access information, and provide feedback without undue delays. Effective communication between leaders and team members, as well as adequate feedback from customers, can enhance an organization's success during a recession.

5.4. Contribution to Knowledge

Both the theoretical and empirical findings of this study contribute to our understanding of the interplay between human resource management and organizational survival, as moderated by organizational culture. This study also enhances our understanding of how public agencies in Rivers State practice and apply their human resource management initiatives.

The findings suggest that the institutionalization of human resource management is more likely when HRM is integrated within the core cultural framework of the organization. Consequently, the likelihood of an initiative being adopted and effectively utilized increases when it is recognized and supported by all key members of the organization, based on its institutionalization within the broader organizational network.

The methodological contribution of this study relates to the appropriateness of applying theoretical concepts and models developed in other contexts. The applicability of research theories and models from developed countries to studies in a developing country like Nigeria has been questioned due to differences in social and cultural settings.

The successful application of these theories in this study provides valuable examples of how research from developing countries, such as Nigeria, can be interpreted using these theoretical frameworks.

One of the practical contributions of this research is the detailed insight provided into the examined public agencies. The case studies reveal that human resource management practices should be linked to organizational change and adaptive behavior. This implies that, for effective implementation, emphasis should be placed on understanding the social contexts of work, tasks, and organizational dynamics. Doing so will help enhance the social integration of human resource management and, hopefully, its institutionalization.

The conceptual and operational framework, along with the heuristic model contributions of this research, will help public agencies gain a competitive edge and position themselves better for long-term survival.

5.5. Limitations of the Study

The study has two main categories of limitations:

- Difficulties in interpreting the SPSS version 22 results.
- Minor errors in form-filling, caused by the absent-mindedness of some respondents.

5.6. Suggestions for Future Studies

This study focused on the relationship between human resource management and organizational survival, particularly within public agencies in Rivers State. As a result, the generalizability of its findings is limited to the specific population studied. It is, therefore, recommended that similar studies, even on the same variables, be conducted in different contexts and industries, such as the private sector—including manufacturing, banking and finance, oil and gas, among others. This would provide a more comprehensive understanding of the relationship between these variables.

Furthermore, related studies could explore areas such as the impact of reward management systems on employee turnover intentions, the role of information technology in enhancing organizational survival, and the moderating effects of contextual variables such as organizational structure, technology, or size. These avenues could provide valuable insights for future research.

References

i. Antonites, A. J. (2003). *An action learning approach to entrepreneurial creativity, innovation and opportunity finding.* (Unpublished doctoral dissertation). University of Pretoria.

ii. Aristotle. (1999a). *Nicomachean ethics* (W. D. Ross, Trans.). Kitchener, Ontario: Batoche Books.

iii. Cropley, A. J., & Urban, K. K. (2000). Programs and strategies for nurturing creativity. In K. A. Heller, F. J. Mönks, R. J. Sternberg, & R. F. Subotnik (Eds.), *International handbook of giftedness and talent* (pp. 481-494). Oxford: Pergamon.

iv. Crovitz, H. F. (1970). *Galton's walk: Methods for the analysis of thinking, intelligence, and creativity.* New York: Harper and Row Publishers.

v. De Bono, E. (1992). *Serious creativity: Using the power of lateral thinking to create new ideas.* Toronto: HarperCollins.

vi. De Bono, E. (1995). Serious creativity. *The Journal for Quality and Participation, 18,* 12-18.

vii. Eysenck, H. J. (2008). *Genius: The natural history of creativity.* Cambridge: Cambridge University Press.

viii. Fillis, I. (2006). Art for art's sake or art for business sake: An exploration of artistic product orientation. *The Marketing Review, 6*(1), 29-40.

ix. Fillis, I., & Rentschler, R. (2010). The role of creativity in entrepreneurship. *Journal of Enterprising Culture, 18*(1), 49-81.

x. Gardner, H. (1988). Creativity: An interdisciplinary perspective. *Creativity Research Journal, 1*(1), 8-26.

xi. Guilford, J. (1951). Creativity. *American Psychologist, 5,* 444-454.

xii. Lubart, T. I. (1994). *Product-centered self-evaluation and the creative process.* (Unpublished doctoral dissertation). Yale University, New Haven, CT.

xiii. Puccio, G. J. (1991). William Duff's eighteenth-century examination of original genius and its relationship to contemporary creativity research. *Journal of Creative Behavior, 25*(1), 1-10.

xiv. Rothenberg, A., & Hausman, C. R. (1976). *The creativity question.* Durham, N.C.: Duke University Press.

xv. Sternberg, R. J. (2006a). Introduction. In J. C. Kaufman & R. J. Sternberg (Eds.), *The international handbook of creativity* (pp. 1-10). New York: Cambridge University Press.

xvi. Sternberg, R. J. (2006b). The nature of creativity. *Creativity Research Journal, 18*(1), 87-98.

xvii. Torrance, E. P. (1994). *Creativity: Just wanting to know.* Pretoria: Benedic Books.

xviii. Torrance, E. P. (1995). *Why fly: A philosophy of creativity.* Norwood, NJ: Ablex Publishing Corporation.

xix. Ward, T. B., Finke, R. A., & Smith, S. M. (1995). *Creativity and the mind: Discovering the genius within.* New York: Plenum Press.

xx. Allan, R. (2017, May 30). The intense corporate 'Hell Camps' of 1980s Japan. *Atlas Obscura.* Retrieved from https://www.atlasobscura.com/articles/hell-camp-japan-80s

xxi. International Monetary Fund. (2020). COVID-19 induces deep global recession. *VOA News.* Retrieved from https://www.voanews.com/economy-business/covid-19-induces-deep-global-recession-2020-says-imf

xxii. Market Business News. (n.d.). Organizational change: Definition & meaning. Retrieved from https://marketbusinessnews.com/financial-glossary/organizational-change-definition-meaning

xxiii. Nairametrics. (2020, November 23). Nigeria to exit recession by first quarter of 2021. Retrieved from https://nairametrics.com/2020/11/23/nigeria-to-exit-recession-by-first-quarter-of-2021/

xxiv. National Bureau of Economic Research. (2020). COVID-19 research papers. Retrieved from https://www.nber.org/wp_covid19.html

xxv. People Magazine. (1988, May 30). A 13-day Japanese boot camp shows U.S. executives how to succeed in business through suffering. Retrieved from https://people.com/archive/a-13-day-japanese-boot-camp-shows-u-s-executives-how-to-succeed-in-business-through-suffering-vol-29-no-21/

xxvi. Plant Services. (2011). Human capital leadership power. Retrieved from https://www.plantservices.com/articles/2011/06-human-capital-leadership-power/

xxvii. World Bank. (2020, June 8). COVID-19 to plunge global economy into worst recession since World War II. Retrieved from https://www.worldbank.org/en/news/press-release/2020/06/08/covid-19-to-plunge-global-economy-into-worst-recession-since-world-war-ii

www.ingramcontent.com/pod-product-compliance
Lightning Source LLC
Chambersburg PA
CBHW050017170726
48282CB00025B/434
* 9 7 8 9 3 4 8 8 9 2 4 9 2 *